Modern American Profiles

Modern American Profiles

Lucette Rollet Kenan

Harcourt Brace Jovanovich, Inc.
New York Chicago San Francisco Atlanta

ISBN: 0-15-559866-X

Library of Congress Catalog Card Number: 74-25381

Printed in the United States of America

Cover illustration by Richard Kluga

Picture Credits

page

1	UPI
10	NASA
19	Alfred Eisenstaedt, from Time-LIFE Picture Agency
27	Wide World
40	Don Uhrbrock, from Time-LIFE Picture Agency
41	Eve Arnold, © 1969 Magnum Photos
53	UPI
67, 74	Ken Heyman
83	Henri Cartier-Bresson, Magnum Photos
95	U.S. Army
117	Elliott Erwitt, © 1968 Magnum Photos
125	Hans Namuth
128	Collection, The Museum of Modern Art, New York, Purchase
134	Private collection
143	Ken Heyman
148	from *Blackberry Winter* by Margaret Mead, Wm. Morrow & Co., New York, 1972
155	Theodore Schwartz
163	Werner Bischof, Magnum Photos
174	Hedrich-Blessing, Chicago
177	The Solomon R. Guggenheim Museum
187	Wide World
199, 200	UPI

Preface

This group of *Modern American Profiles* is intended for students who would like to improve their proficiency in reading English. The primary objective of the book is to provide material of real interest that can be read with ease and pleasure. Each of its ten chapters offers one or more informal portraits of prominent Americans who represent a broad spectrum of backgrounds, interests, and accomplishments—scientists and black leaders, entertainers and artists, a writer, an astronaut, and the members of a famous political family—all contemporary, significant, and exciting, and almost all controversial.

The style of *Modern American Profiles* is the lively modern English the reader is likely to encounter in American newspapers and periodicals and in everyday conversation. Colorful words, constructions, and colloquialisms found in contemporary English appear in the text, with explanatory glosses and notes. In most cases these terms are used in the vocabulary and grammar exercises following each profile and reappear in later chapters. Although the writing has been kept simple enough throughout to be easily understood by anyone with a moderate command of English, students are encouraged to sharpen their facility with the language: as the book progresses, the style and vocabulary become increasingly difficult.

Flexibility has been a major goal of the book. Depending on the format of the course, the competence of the students, and the time available to them, the profiles can be used for short or long assignments. They can be read aloud or silently in class, or, for instructors who wish to emphasize conversation, they can be assigned as outside reading to be discussed in class. Parts of the text can serve as a basis for dictation or as material for student writing. Although the important people and events mentioned in the profiles have been identified in footnotes and glosses, students who have access to a reference library can research these topics and perhaps make oral presentations or write short papers on their findings.

In the interest of flexibility, each profile is divided into two or three units of five to seven pages each. Following the profile, a series of exercises has been provided for each separate unit to test students' comprehension and to help them expand their vocabulary and gain familiarity with sentence structure. Each group of exercises ends with a list of suggested topics for discussion that can be used partially or even totally for written assignments. The list is not meant to be exhaustive; instructors and students may choose to develop some of the suggested topics further or to discuss others of their own.

In any event, it is recommended that students be encouraged to ask questions, to comment, to criticize—in short, to discuss freely the personalities and fields of activity presented in the profiles. In this way students can not only improve their proficiency in reading and in expressing themselves but broaden their knowledge of important contemporary figures, problems, and events in the United States.

L. R. K.

Contents

Neil Alden Armstrong

O n July 16, 1969, Apollo XI was launched° at Cape   set in motion
Kennedy Space Center, Florida. It was carrying three men: Neil
Armstrong, the commander of the flight, who would be the first
man to walk on the moon; Edwin (Buzz) Aldrin, who would
follow him there; and Michael Collins, who would have to wait
for his companions in the space ship without landing at all.
Without any doubt, this was a great date in the history of
mankind. Millions of people all over the world were following
the event; three thousand journalists were covering it in dozens
of languages, doing their best to provide the public with
learned scientific details, enthusiastic comments, and exciting
stories about the three human stars of the adventure.

Many reporters and writers met with the astronauts before
the trip; but those who interviewed Neil Armstrong emerged°   came out of
from the experience puzzled and sometimes annoyed. Not that
he had been unpleasant or impatient. Not at all. Talking to the
press is part of an astronaut's job, just like flying T-38 jets to
keep the reflexes° sharp, or learning what kind of snakes to eat   automatic reactions
if you are ever lost in Borneo. It is a duty, and Neil Armstrong is
not the kind of man who neglects his duties.

What was it, then, that bothered the reporters? Here was their
man, who soon would be the first human being to disturb the
lunar° dust—or sink in it; our Hero, our Pride, our Explorer,   of the moon
the Pioneer of the Technological Age, ready to launch into
space with all the dreams and fears of humanity:

"Mr. Armstrong, becoming an astronaut must have given you
a great joy?
—I was already a test pilot for NASA. To me it was simply
being transferred from one office to another.
—Do you mean you don't have a taste for adventure?
—For heaven's sake, I hate danger. Danger is the most
annoying aspect of our job. . . . How can a simple
technological fact be turned into an adventure?
—But I suppose you would be sorry not to go up?
—Yes, but I would not get sick about it. I don't understand
those who get so anxious to be first. It's all nonsense, just
romanticism unworthy of our rational age.

—I know somebody who would go up even if he knew that he would not come back. . . .

—He is a child, not an adult. I would not agree to go up if I thought I might not come back. Unless it were technically necessary. Testing a jet is dangerous but technically necessary. Dying in space or on the moon is not necessary, and so if I had to choose, I'd choose death while testing a jet. Wouldn't you?

—No, I'd choose to die on the moon; at least I would have seen it. . . .

—Nonsense! If it were a matter of staying there for a year or two, perhaps . . . no, no; it would be too high a price to pay. Because it is senseless! I'd better say goodbye now. I have to go into the centrifuge.[1]

—I don't envy you, Mr. Armstrong.

—Yes, it is unpleasant. Perhaps the thing I hate most. But it is necessary. . . ." [2]

And so it went. No wonder many reporters found him depressing. Besides, it seemed impossible to sell him to the public. How do you make a folk hero of a man who is unwilling to play the part; who stubbornly defends his privacy, does not answer personal questions, refuses to make any philosophic or poetic declaration about his mission, and does not even kiss his wife for the cameras, as a good folk hero should? He seemed determined to look as uninteresting as he could. And yet he aroused his visitors' curiosity. There was a disturbing intensity° in that stiff Boy Scout with the lopsided° smile and the wary° blue eyes, so shy at thirty-nine that he blushed and stammered° when forced to speak in public. Norman Mailer, who was observing the launching of Apollo XI for *Life* magazine, wrote uncomfortably that Armstrong "was just not like other men. He was a presence in the room, a spirit as much as a man . . . extraordinarily remote,° with something particularly innocent or faintly sinister° in the gentle remote air. He was in communication with strings° in the Universe that others did not think to play."

If this description seems fanciful, it fits well nonetheless. Neil Armstrong is indeed a remote man, partly because he wants to keep himself beyond the reach of curious strangers,

depth; strength of feeling / crooked

cautious

spoke haltingly

seeming far away

bad, evil

here, of a musical instrument (fig.)

[1] A machine to accustom the astronauts to the stress of acceleration.
[2] Interview with Neil Armstrong by Italian journalist Oriana Fallaci.

Neil Alden Armstrong

and partly because he has been "in communication with the Universe" for most of his life. He was only two years old when his father took him to the Cleveland airport to watch some air races. Four years later Stephen Armstrong gave his small son his first ride in an old twin-engine plane. It can be said that Neil never really came back from that ride. Nothing afterward excited him as much as flight and aircraft. He read all he could find on the subject, collected information on the characteristics and performance of all types of planes, built models, and learned to fly before he even thought of driving a car. As a pilot, his favorite way of relaxing from testing jets was to go soaring° in a glider,° and gliding is still his only sport.

It is difficult to believe that a man with such a passion could have remained as cool as Armstrong appeared during the last days before takeoff.° But it would have been out of character° for him to show his true feelings. He never does; he never talks about himself—never talks at all if he can help it. Even at home he protects his peace and privacy behind a wall of silence. "Silence," says his wife, "is a Neil Armstrong answer. The word *no* is an argument."° His two sons complain that he never answers their questions, and his friends admit that they have no hope of ever knowing exactly what he thinks. But all agree that he is a pleasant, undemanding man, incredibly° patient and easy to live with—as long as you do not insist on conversation.

From all reports, he is a good family man, a good companion, a good citizen, a good man altogether. And why not? In Wapakoneta, where he comes from, there is no disgrace in trying to be good, to think straight, to obey the rules. People there work hard and admire economy and modesty. But they are not timid° souls. They have never been afraid to go into unknown territory to clear new farms or to reach new frontiers. They would not hesitate to explore another planet, given the chance. So it was not extraordinary for Neil Armstrong to practice the old-fashioned American virtues while pursuing° his own dream and to find his balance, so to speak, with one foot in the grassroots° of America and the other one in science fiction.

With its seven thousand inhabitants, Wapakoneta, Ohio, is a typical, small American town—friendly, sensible, busy. "People in this community," explained Armstrong to a journalist, "believed that it was important to do a useful job

Margin glosses:

soaring° flying high

glider,° a plane without an engine, carried by air currents

takeoff.° launching/out

character° . . . not like him

argument."° quarrel; discussion

incredibly° unbelievably

timid° easily afraid

pursuing° following

grassroots° in . . . among the ordinary people *(fig.)*

4

and to do it well." Since his father's job (checking the records of state agencies) kept the family moving every year, Neil did not actually grow up in Wapakoneta, but in other small towns similar to it. The Armstrongs came back to their home town when Neil was in high school.

The three Armstrong children were brought up strictly but lovingly by their mother, a serious woman with a fondness for books and music. Neil soon shared her tastes. He was the best-read° young man in first grade, and he has never stopped reading since. He loves music, any kind of music from popular to classical; he played the horn in the school band, is still an acceptable pianist, and when he is in a relaxed mood he will sometimes play funny duets° with his wife to entertain his friends.

"I am afraid that I did a lot of ordinary things in my youth," he said to the newsmen covering° Apollo XI. And it is true that he was a very normal boy with ordinary friends and activities. But those activities did not hold his interest as much as they could have. He did become a Boy Scout like his pals; but he did not bother to work for his Eagle Scout badge[3] until he was in college. He did not care for sports and still does not. In Houston, among the astronauts, he was to make himself conspicuous° by refusing to do the push-ups,° the jogging,° and the other exercises so dear to his colleagues.° A man has only so many heartbeats in his lifetime, he thinks, and he does not intend to waste his on gymnastics.° As a boy, Neil could be persuaded to play ball, if only to please his friends. But he did not stay on the field any longer than he had to. He was much happier in his cluttered° room full of technical magazines and adventure books, with airplane models dangling° from the ceiling. He could go to the basement of his house where his mother had let him build a wind tunnel.[4] Often he would run to his neighbor's telescope and look into the sky for a long time. He may have allowed himself to daydream° a bit; at least he did have a recurring° nighttime dream of being able to hover° above the ground by holding his breath. He tried it once when awake with disappointing results.

Neil did well in school, as could be expected from a young man with a purpose; luckily, he shone in subjects that were

who has read the most

pieces of music for two players or singers

reporting on

easily noticed, attracting attention/ a type of physical exercise / slow run
co-workers

physical exercises

overcrowded

hanging down

imagine situations
repeated regularly/float

[3]A special pin showing the highest rank of Boy Scout.
[4]A structure in which the effects of different winds on model aircraft are studied.

Neil Alden Armstrong

right for his future career—mathematics and science. He still had time after school to play his horn in the band, to study calculus,° and to earn some money. Where he lived, children were encouraged to go to work at an early age—it was the natural thing to do. At seven Neil was mowing° the grass in the cemetery for ten cents an hour. Later he made as much as forty cents an hour working in local stores, making doughnuts in a bakery, or helping the mechanics at the local airfield. He saved all his earnings very patiently; it took a long time to collect the nine dollars that would pay for an hour of flying instruction. As soon as he had the money, Neil ran to the airport. On his sixteenth birthday—the first day it was legal—he received his pilot's license. If anything could have stopped him from becoming a flyer it would have been at that time, when another student pilot, a friend of his, was killed in his plane. But after two days in his room, Neil came out with his plans unchanged.

Thanks to his good grades in high school, Neil received a scholarship from the Navy. Since the rules provided that he could choose a university instead of the Naval Academy, he selected Purdue, which was offering excellent courses in aeronautical engineering.° The Navy claimed him anyway, after a year and a half; it sent him first to Florida for pilot training and then to Korea, where the war had started. Armstrong was the youngest man in a jet squadron° attached to the carrier *Essex.* When the war ended, he was twenty-one years old; he had flown seventy-eight missions and had won three medals, as well as a reputation as a "hot"° pilot with a cool head. The cool head had saved his life twice: once he had managed to coax° his damaged jet back to the carrier; another time he had somehow flown long enough with a broken wing to reach friendly territory, where he was rescued promptly after parachuting to the ground. He has faced death many times since, without ever losing his poise.

During his leaves from Korea Neil discovered Japan, and he was so enchanted by its culture that he became positively eloquent° on the subject. Back in Purdue after his discharge from the Navy, he went so far as to write the lyrics and music for a "Japanese" variety show that was presented on campus. After that frivolous° affair, however, he went back to work seriously for his bachelor's degree—but not without keeping an eye on Janet Shearon, a physical education student with a fine figure and a passion for swimming. Better yet, she knew

a branch of mathematics

cutting with a machine

the science of designing, making, and flying planes

jet . . . . military unit of jet planes

here, very eager

persuade

speaking well and persuasively

not serious

something about planes, for her father had owned one. But even such remarkable qualities were not sufficient to hurry matters. It took Armstrong two years to ask Janet for a date. ("Neil never rushes into anything," she says.) They were eventually married in January 1956.

II

At the time of his marriage, Neil Armstrong had his master's degree and was already a test pilot for the National Aeronautics and Space Administration (NASA) at Edwards Air Force Base in southern California. For several years—"the most fascinating years of my life!"—he tested all sorts of experimental aircraft, including the rocket-powered X-15, which could fly at over five thousand miles per hour at the edge of the atmosphere. The X-15 was used to study flight in a thin atmosphere, the effect of air resistance on high-speed planes, and other similar problems. "We were doing exciting, way-out° things," says Armstrong. "We were not just pilots; we were engineers and developers of programs, using planes merely as tools, the way an astronomer° uses a telescope." The main object of the research was to prepare men and machines for space travel, an adventure in which Armstrong was passionately eager to participate. He knew, of course, that somewhere in New Mexico a group of engineers were playing with rockets under the guidance° of German experts; but he could not take them seriously. As he saw it, space would be explored by winged aircraft. They needed only to be perfected, and he was devoting himself to perfecting them.

While Neil was happily flying his machines, Janet was keeping house° in the wilderness. Typically, instead of settling near Edwards Air Force Base with the other pilots' families, the Armstrongs had preferred to buy a former ranger's° cabin, five thousand feet up in the mountains. Quite a home, Armstrong remembers fondly. It had no plumbing,° no electricity, and no hot water. But who cared about such small matters? The view was splendid, the privacy absolute, and, after all, Janet could let the sun warm up the baby's bath in the backyard. She did not risk upsetting any neighbors when she climbed on the roof with her binoculars° to watch her husband flash by, wagging° the tail of his plane at her. In the course of seven years, two

extraordinary, odd

scientist who studies the heavenly bodies

direction

keeping . . . taking care of the household

man paid to guard an area

pipes carrying water and refuse

small telescope for both eyes / moving in greeting (dog *wags* his tail)

children were born, and the plumbing was installed. Then it was time to move.

The year was 1962. A Russian and an American had flown around the earth in rockets. Congress, suddenly anxious to send a man to the moon, had voted the necessary funds, and at the Manned Spacecraft Center in Houston, work on the Gemini project was well under way.° Finally convinced that NASA was °in process getting serious, Armstrong applied for training as an astronaut and was promptly accepted. He was to remain the only civilian pilot in the program.

Neil and Janet moved to a proper suburb of Houston, near the Center, and, for the first time since their marriage, adjusted to a conventional way of life. They followed the almost-military customs of the astronauts' community, submitted to interviews, and attended parties where Neil, too shy to thaw° easily, °melt spent most of the time in a quiet corner. With his passion for privacy, his unlisted telephone number, his books, his music, his lonely gliding, Armstrong never impressed his fellow astronauts as the most sociable personality around. Janet fitted better. She met the wives, participated in their activities, and was properly seen in church on Sundays. Considering his upbringing, one assumes that Armstrong is a fine Christian. But he keeps his religious beliefs so much to himself that at one time he was suspected of being a Buddhist, perhaps because of his well-known admiration for Japan. Besides, he had built an Oriental-looking house for his family and installed a large Buddha in the living room. But he explained reasonably to an inquiring visitor that a true Buddhist house would have had the main beam painted red to frighten the evil spirits away. Apparently he should have painted his beam, for the house burned one night, and although he saved his children, he lost in the fire his precious collection of old *Air Trails* magazines.

To fill her lonely hours, Janet taught physical education and swimming. She had plenty of time to kill;° an astronaut is not °time . . . free time home much. Like his colleagues, Armstrong had to travel often. He had to make publicity trips throughout the country—to the different companies that were building the parts of the spacecraft; to the launching Center at Cape Kennedy; to Arizona to study Meteor Crater[5] with geologists and to rehearse° °practice the lunar landing on a "lunar landscape." There were splash-down° rehearsals in the Gulf of Mexico and survival °falling into the sea

[5]A large hole in the earth caused by the falling of a fragment from space.

training in the desert. There were endless lectures on geology,° [science of rocks and terrains] astronomy, lunography,° [study of the moon's surface/] meteorology,° [science of atmosphere and weather] photography, television technics;° [practical methods/] on the complicated equipment of the capsule° [cabin of the spacecraft] and on the anatomy° and manipulation° of the computers. [structure/ handling, working] There were hours and hours in the centrifuge and in the vacuum chamber[6]; hours flying helicopters and jets; hours in the simulator, an enormous contraption° [queer-looking machine] where the sights, sounds, motions, and accidents of a space flight are simulated while instructors watch the reactions of the astronauts. The computers can produce seventeen hundred different "crises."° [dangerous moments]

This hard training was meant to prepare the astronauts and their spacecraft for the demands of space exploration. Every piece of equipment was tested and retested; every stage of the operation was rehearsed many times. The previous missions had gradually smoothed the way. In the Mercury capsules (carrying one man) and in the Gemini capsules (carrying two men), the astronauts had accustomed themselves to live and work in zero gravity,° [weightlessness] to walk in space, to recover packages launched separately, to link two spacecraft together. They had orbited, inspected, and photographed the moon. In May 1966, Apollo X had circled very close to the lunar surface. The only part of the Apollo XI expedition that had not been and could not be rehearsed was the takeoff of the Lunar Module (the LM) from the moon at the end of the mission. The LM itself had been tested many times; Armstrong almost lost his life during one of the tests. The machine went out of control, and he barely had time to jump off with his parachute seconds before the LM crashed in flames.

Danger—that "annoying aspect of the job"—was always present. All astronauts accepted it calmly, and Armstrong was, according to an English journalist, "the ultimate° [highest level] in calm." He never panicked.° [was confused by fear] He had not panicked in Korea, in the crashing LM, or in the burning of his house, and he had even kept a clear head in Gemini 8 when a wild thruster[7] had made the capsule carrying him and David Scott tumble end over end. As the motion was increasing and the technicians in Houston were wondering if the astronauts would lose consciousness, Armstrong's quiet voice announced: "We consider the problem serious." Whereupon° [after which] he had pushed the button starting reentry° [coming back to earth] operations—the only move, it was calculated later,

[6]A machine to accustom the astronauts to the lack of atmosphere.
[7]The part of the rocket engine that discharges gas, pushing the capsule ahead.

Neil Alden Armstrong 9

Apollo XI astronaut Edwin Aldrin on the moon, July 20, 1969.

that could have saved the craft and the crew. Gemini 8 splashed undamaged into the Pacific. As for the landing of Apollo XI on the moon, it would have ended in disaster° if Armstrong had not taken control of the operation when he realized that the overworked computer was guiding the LM to the bottom of a crater full of huge rocks. He piloted the module farther and

ruin

made it land with just enough fuel left for forty seconds of flight, demonstrating at that moment why machines may not be able to replace men entirely in the exploration of the universe.

There was at least one man in Houston who knew that Neil Armstrong's celebrated calm covered the most fragile° nerves and the wildest heart on Apollo XI. That man was Dr. Charles Berry, the NASA physician attending° the astronauts. He had seen Armstrong's heartbeat rate (normal at 77 beats per minute) climb to 106 during the smooth takeoff, while Collins' rate was remaining reasonably at 90, and Aldrin's was almost normal at 80. When the LM touched the lunar surface, Armstrong's heart was thumping° 156 times per minute. The newsmen, who had judged him a cold fish,° made so much of that fact that Armstrong showed annoyance. He must have been even more displeased when Dr. Berry told the press that the "remote" astronaut was a rather emotional man—and when his mother added that he had been crying on the moon. These are not the kinds of things that he likes to see revealed. It was even mentioned that, in a rare display of sentimentality,° he had carried into space pieces of fabric from the first airplane to fly around the world (in 1924); he also had taken the watch of the aviator who had tried, and failed, to repeat the flight alone in 1933.

What becomes of an astronaut after he has come back to earth; when he has answered all the questions of the scientists and technicians; when he is through with the celebrations, the parades, the interviews, the dinners, the lecture tours, and the trips abroad; when the noise has died away? Neither the engineer-astronauts nor the scientist-astronauts can easily resume their original careers which have been interrupted for too long by the years of specialized training at NASA. What do they do? Some succeed in business: Alan Shepard is now a bank president and a millionaire; Frank Borman is vice president of the transportation division of an airline company. Others have chosen a new kind of adventure: Don Eisele leads the Peace Corps in Thailand; Scott Carpenter is head of an oceanographic° company. Others have found it difficult to readjust. Dependable° Buzz Aldrin, "the man who could correct computers," barely avoided a nervous breakdown and had to seek psychiatric help. Several unwise astronauts have ruined their careers in the Air Force or the Navy by selling souvenirs and stamped envelopes brought back from the moon.

Such misfortune would not happen to Neil Armstrong. He

easily damaged, delicate

in charge of

beating strongly
cold . . . person who has no feelings (fam.)

display of emotion

studying the oceans

to be trusted, relied on

certainly has a healthy interest in money, and he keeps a sharp eye on his investments.° But he would not get involved in questionable° deals. In fact, he does not even capitalize° on his fame in a legitimate° way, and he seldom accepts payment for his lectures on moon exploration.

business in which he has put his money
of doubtful honesty/ make money out of
proper

After the Apollo mission, Neil Armstrong became Deputy Assistant Administrator of Aeronautics at NASA's headquarters in Washington. For a year or so he supervised research in such areas as traffic control, control of engine noise, and wing safety and efficiency. But a desk job is dull, even for a sensible astronaut, and in October 1971 Armstrong left NASA to become a professor of aeronautical engineering at the University of Cincinnati in Ohio. He avoids publicity, refuses to give any interviews, and lives quietly between his family and his students. He seems to have made a wise choice for his second career, since he remains in his field and can now pass on to younger men his enthusiasm and his superb knowledge of aeronautics. "The single thing which makes man happiest," he says, "is the feeling that he has worked up to the limit of his ability; it is all the better if this work has made a contribution to knowledge or toward moving the human race a little farther ahead." Although he is not a conceited° man with a grandiose° view of himself, Armstrong must feel that he has made his contribution and deserved his happiness. How happy he actually is in a life that is now bound to earth is anybody's guess. It is a question on which he remains, of course, silent.

vain/
very great

Questions

1. Why was the Apollo XI mission particularly exciting?
2. What impression did you have of Neil Armstrong after reading his interview with Oriana Fallaci?
3. Why did Oriana Fallaci say, "I don't envy you, Mr. Armstrong"?
4. What impression did he make on Norman Mailer?
5. How would you describe the kind of town where he grew up?
6. Why is it not surprising that an astronaut should have come from there?
7. Do you think that Neil Armstrong was indeed different from his friends, and from most other boys, in his youth?
8. What qualities did he display during the Korean War?
9. How did he show his enthusiasm for Japanese culture?
10. What does his marriage to Janet reveal about each of them?

Vocabulary

A   *Repeat the following sentences, replacing the word or phrase in italics with one with similar meaning taken from the list. Adjustments have to be made for the plural of nouns and the tenses of verbs.*

promptly	argument
sinister	dangle
incredibly	wary
pursue	coax
reflex	conspicuous
in character	emerge from
gymnastics	improvise
jog	hover
remote	

1. The reporters were puzzled when they *came out of* the interview.
2. Armstrong was looking at them with *cautious* eyes.
3. He gave them the impression of being *far away.*
4. It would not have been *like him* to show his feelings.
5. He does not like *quarrels.*
6. He always dreamed that he was *floating* above the ground.
7. He is *unbelievably* patient.
8. He was a sensible. boy, but he *followed* his own dreams.
9. His plane models were *hanging down* from the ceiling.
10. He married a physical education major but he does not care for *physical exercises.*

B *Choose the most accurate of the three statements.*

1. A timid man
   a) is very sick
   b) saves his money
   c) is easily afraid

2. A man stammers
   a) because he is shy
   b) because he is amused
   c) because he has missed a step

3. A cluttered room
   a) is locked
   b) is very small
   c) has many things in it

4. He is eloquent about Japan
   a) he dislikes it
   b) he speaks well about it
   c) he does not know the country

5. He loves to soar in his glider
   a) to sing in it
   b) to dive in it
   c) to fly high in it

6. He coaxed his mother into letting him build a wind tunnel
   a) he persuaded her
   b) he tricked her
   c) he forced her

C *Write the antonyms for the following words, using the prefixes* **in-, im-, un-.**

1. pleasant
2. comfortable
3. patient
4. demanding
5. credible
6. lucky
7. possible
8. known
9. worthy

Structure

Example Perhaps he allowed himself to daydream.
          He may have allowed himself to daydream.

1. Perhaps he was as ordinary as he looked.
2. Perhaps they found him too sensible.
3. Perhaps he thought that the journalists were depressing.
4. Perhaps you saw the "moon landing" on television.
5. Perhaps Armstrong's father dreamed of flying, too.
6. Perhaps Collins preferred to stay in the Command Module.
7. Perhaps he ate most of the doughnuts he made.
8. Perhaps he did not dare to ask her for a date.

Topics for Discussion or Written Assignment

1. What folk heroes can you name? What makes a folk hero? Are they necessarily the best in their field? Can you think of some who are not? How do you feel about folk heroes?
2. What sorts of people are likely to be attracted by a career as an astronaut? What sorts of people are fit for it? Why would, or wouldn't, you like to be an astronaut?
3. What impression do you have of Neil Armstrong's father?
4. Do you like science fiction books or films? Why? Have you read or seen any that interested you? Explain.
5. How would you compare your home town with Wapakoneta and its people?
6. What is your idea of a good citizen?

Exercises for Section II *pp. 7-12*

Questions

1. What was Neil Armstrong's first job with NASA?
2. What did he do at Edwards Air Force Base?
3. What was so special about the Armstrongs' first house?
4. What does the choice of that house reveal about their character and their way of life?
5. What led them to leave the house?
6. Why had Neil not been interested in rockets before?
7. What subjects do astronauts have to study?
8. How had the previous missions prepared for the moon landing expedition?

9. What part of the expedition could not be rehearsed? Why?
10. Is Neil Armstrong a cold fish? Explain.

True or False

Explain your choice.

1. A simulator is a place in Arizona that has been made to look like a lunar landscape.
2. Immediately after they came back to earth, the astronauts were very busy.
3. The moon landing was done entirely by computer.
4. Armstrong is not at all interested in money.
5. Aldrin had a hard time after the Apollo XI mission.
6. After the Apollo XI mission, Neil Armstrong became a professor of aeronautical engineering.

Vocabulary

A   *Repeat the following sentences after filling the blanks with the noun suggested by the verb or adjective in italics.*

Example: He *communicates* with the universe.
He is in **communication** with the universe.

1. They showed that they were *annoyed*; they showed their _____.
2. We *flew* for a long time; it was a long _____.
3. Neil never tells anyone what he *believes*; he keeps his _____ to himself.
4. He was *brought up* strictly; he had a strict _____.
5. He learned to *manipulate* the computers; he learned the _____ of the computers.
6. They lived in a *wild* area; they lived in the _____.
7. They were *guided* by several German experts; under their _____ they made the first experiments with rockets.
8. She was *fond* of music, and Neil too had a great _____ for it.
9. Did they *rehearse* well? No, they had a terrible _____.
10. It is just *romantic* fancy, just _____ unworthy of our age.

B   1. What do you call the science of rocks and terrains?
2. What is lunography?
3. What does a ranger do?

4. What do you call the study of atmosphere and weather?
5. What do you call a man who studies heavenly bodies?
6. What is a contraption?
7. What is a crater?
8. What is the purpose of the centrifuge?
9. What is the anatomy of a computer?
10. What is the plumbing of a house?

Structures

A **Example** He became a pilot; then he married Janet.
After he had become a pilot, he married Janet.

1. He finished his book; then he went to play baseball.
2. They installed the plumbing; then they sold the house.
3. She bathed the baby; then she climbed up on the roof.
4. He did twenty push-ups; then he said that he would rather glide.
5. She talked to the astronauts; then she wrote a mean article about them.
6. They landed on the moon; then they refused to leave it.

B **Example** It was a great adventure. He was eager to participate in it.
It was a great adventure **in which** he was eager to participate.

1. There were many interviews. He had to submit to them.
2. A simulator is a huge contraption. The astronauts emerged exhausted from it.
3. There was also a centrifuge. Armstrong did not like to go into it.
4. The X-15 is a special plane. Armstrong experimented with it at Edwards Air Force Base.
5. This is a dangerous mission. They have to be well prepared for it.
6. The capsule is a part of the rocket. The astronauts travel in it.
7. This is the Lunar Module. They landed on the moon with it.

Topics for Discussion or Written Assignment

1. How would you describe Neil Armstrong to someone who did not know anything about him?
2. Would you like to see the space program continued? Is the exploration of the universe a worthwhile project? Is it worth the money spent on it? Why?
3. Should there be women astronauts? Mixed crews? International crews? Defend your answer.

Neil Alden Armstrong

4. Do you think a trip in space can change a man's character, point of view, or religious attitude? Give reasons for your answer.
5. Are there other intelligent beings in the universe? What makes you think the way you do?
6. Neil Armstrong told Oriana Fallaci that he would not go to the moon if he thought he would not come back. She said she would. Would you? Explain your answer.

Marilyn
Monroe

Born June 1, 1926
In Los Angeles, California
Died August 5, 1962

Sex queens come and go, easily crowned, easily forgotten. Yet Marilyn Monroe's memory has remained very much alive. Admirers still cut her picture out of public library books; artists still paint her; even the young have become familiar with her name and her face by watching her films on television. In the summer of 1972, both American and foreign magazines marked the tenth anniversary of her death with kind articles; some of them printed the poems that she had written. Her life had already been researched with great care. It had inspired several biographies, a mediocre° film, and a play *(After the Fall)* by Arthur Miller, who had been her third husband. Miller, having perhaps too candidly° exposed the unpleasant sides of her character in his play, was charged by many people with cruelty, bad taste, and the exploitation° of a famous ghost.

not very good

frankly

use of someone for personal gain

The sympathy of the public was on Marilyn's side, as it had always been, but with an added touch of respect that she would have welcomed during her life. Respect was seldom granted her. In fact, she was so used to being ridiculed that at the end of her last interview she pleaded with the reporter : "Please, don't make me a joke!" Death has changed the sexy blonde into a myth,° a symbol of soft femininity and loveliness, the silk-and-honey dream of an era. With her legend shining like a halo° around her platinum° head, she is sometimes mistaken for a saintly martyr,° which she certainly was not. But then, what was she?

imaginary being or story

circle of light /
here, pale blonde

one who suffers much for a cause

Those who knew her disagree so violently that it is difficult to see the real woman through the conflicting judgments of her friends and enemies. A simple little girl to her first husband, the biggest con artist° of them all to producer Mike Todd, she has also been described as the most unappreciated person in the world, the meanest woman in Hollywood, a tart,° an enchanting child, an idiot, a wit, a great natural intelligence, a victim, and a cold "user" of people. From the very contradictions, one can guess that she was not simple. And obviously she had something special—not talent, perhaps, but a certain spark. After remarking bitterly, "I have never met anyone as utterly mean as Marilyn Monroe," Billy Wilder, who had

con . . . swindler, deceiver

prostitute

directed her in two films, felt obliged to add, "nor as utterly fabulous° on screen—and that includes Garbo." It was Marilyn's private tragedy that, once at the top, she could not cope with° her fame. It all ended on the night of August 5, 1962, when she swallowed a handful of sleeping pills and died alone in the house that she had just bought in order to start—once more—a new life.

unbelievably good, beautiful

cope . . . handle

It is well known that most of her problems had their roots in an unhappy childhood. It may not, however, have been as brutal as advertised by Marilyn, who had plenty of imagination and a superb sense of publicity. She told the press that she had become an orphan at birth, had grown up in a series of terrible foster homes,° and had been raped° in one of them at the age of twelve. Or was it at six? Or at nine? She also claimed that she could remember her grandmother trying to smother° her under a pillow when she was one year old—a remarkable feat of memory, to say the least.

homes for children without parents / forced to submit to sexual relations

kill by depriving of air

The truth would have been sad enough. Marilyn had come into the world in a Los Angeles hospital as Norma Jean Mortensen, daughter of a film splicer° named Gladys Monroe Mortensen. The baby was carrying a tragic family history. Her mother, her grandmother, her grandfather, and one uncle suffered from paranoid schizophrenia,° and they all died in mental institutions. Despite their delicate beauty, the women of the family seemed unable to keep their men. Gladys had had two bad marriages before her affair with Norma Jean's father, who was another employee of the film studio. Norma Jean, forever anxious to find affection, tried to meet her father when she was a starlet.° His refusal to see her deepened her already sharp feeling of worthlessness.

person who cuts and adjusts movie films

paranoid . . . a severe mental illness

young actress being trained to be a star

Gladys loved her child; but since she had to work, she left her in the hands of Ida and Albert Bolender, a respectable couple who boarded° children on their farm. Norma Jean spent her first seven years with them. Her physical needs were well looked after, and Gladys visited faithfully every weekend. But when she had gone, there was not much warmth around the little girl. The Bolenders were austerely° religious people, rather too severe with a mischievous child. Worse yet, they kept reminding her that she was not a member of their family. For Norma Jean, who was extremely sensitive, it was a lonely, distressing childhood.

supplied food and lodging for pay

very strictly, sternly

In 1933 Gladys bought a house and took her daughter home

with her. But she was not there much, and when she was out, Norma Jean had to stay with the elderly couple who rented part of the house. They were not bad people, only indifferent and more interested in drinking than in baby-sitting. When Norma Jean did not have to go to school, the couple dropped her at a nearby movie house in time for the first afternoon show. The little girl watched happily all day, and after the last matinee° [afternoon show] she walked home by herself, pondering° the adventures of the [thinking deeply about] hero and heroine of the film. In her room, later, she would act out the whole story. In this way she developed a passion for acting that she never outgrew. With everybody around her involved in moviemaking (even the elderly tenant was a stand-in°) it is not at all surprising that the girl should have [substitute for an actor] patterned her dreams, as well as her idea of life, elegance, and happiness, on the make-believe world of film.

After nine months of this "togetherness," Gladys had a mental collapse and was hospitalized. She was to reappear from time to time in her daughter's life, but more as a burden than as a support. After her mother's hospitalization, Norma Jean was sent to an orphanage. She seemed to adapt reasonably well, but in her second year there she tried to run away, and the directress° decided to put her in a foster home in the hope that [woman in charge] she would feel happier in more normal surroundings. The experiment proved disastrous. Other homes were tried. After the third one, the bright, fun-loving girl from the Bolender farm [person who avoids other people / examining her own thoughts] had turned into a loner° silent, introspective,° and totally insecure.° Her life, she believed, was of no interest to anybody. [feeling unsure, unprotected] She was worthless, unwanted. No amount of love or public adulation° was ever to cure her of that conviction. [extravagant praise]

She had never been entirely friendless during those three dark years, however. Her mother's former boss, Grace McKee, had volunteered to be Norma Jean's guardian. She saw her often and took her to the movies, to restaurants, and to the beauty parlor for her first hairset. Finally, she took her into her own home. From the ages of eleven to sixteen, Norma Jean lived either with Grace or with Grace's Aunt Ana, to whom she was very devoted. To please Ana she became a Christian Scientist, just as later she would study Judaism° for the sake of [Jewish religion] Arthur Miller and his father. Norma Jean would have done almost anything to fit more closely into the lives of those she loved.

As a teen-ager Norma Jean seemed happy enough. She was

good in her studies and loved literature and sports: the future sex goddess was a tomboy.° But at fourteen she was beginning to look so splendidly feminine that her pals lost interest in her skill at sports, and Norma Jean realized that nature had provided her with wonderful means to make friends and influence people.

Shortly after her sixteenth birthday, she married a young neighbor, Jim Dougherty. Jim now remembers her as a hard-working housekeeper and an uncertain cook. They only had three years together until Jim was sent to war in 1945. His bride took a job in the parachute department of a defense plant. There, one day, she caught the eye of an Army photographer who had come to make a film called *Women in the War Effort*. It was immediately obvious to that man that he could make the war effort fascinating by showing Norma Jean along with the machines. What he had not foreseen° was that the charming girl with the glorious figure and a weak chin would turn out to be a photographer's dream. Not only did her skin catch the light in the most beautiful way, but she understood photography; she did not have to be told how to move or how to sit. After three days of picture-taking, he advised her to forget the parachutes and to try her chance at modeling.° He helped her find an agency where she could be trained while working at modeling jobs. Without any hesitation Norma Jean left the plant and the house of her parents-in-law, with whom she had been living. The manager of the agency, who had taken her under her wing,° did her best to keep Norma Jean steadily employed.

II

Many people were to take Norma Jean under their wings throughout the years. She looked so insecure, so defenseless, and so vague that men and women alike felt compelled to protect the lamb lost in the jungle. Agents and acting instructors, studio executives and make-up assistants, actors, actresses, poets, husbands, and ordinary people—she always found protectors. Not everybody saw her as a lamb, however. Many people insisted that under all that endearing helplessness, Norma Jean hid the jaws of a barracuda.° They believed that her lonely childhood had made her totally self-centered° and had taught her to charm and use those who could advance her career. Furthermore, they pointed out that she was prompt to dismiss° the protectors who had ceased to be helpful to her. It may be that she dismissed them only when she fancied that they had failed or betrayed her.

°send away

The first to be dismissed was Jim Dougherty. However vague Norma Jean may have been about life in general, she never felt vague about the career she wanted to have. Modeling was only a first step; she wanted to be an actress. Since there was no room for Jim in that future, she wrote him in the spring of 1946 that she was filing for divorce. Then she presented herself bravely to the director of the casting department° of Twentieth-Century Fox studios, Ben Lyons. The experienced Lyons decided that such luminous° skin deserved a test in full color. When the head of the studio, Darryl Zanuck, saw the result, he had Norma Jean admitted forthwith° into the ranks of Fox starlets. At that time Ben Lyons suggested a change of name. He saw her as a "Marilyn." She added her mother's maiden name, and they both agreed that "Marilyn Monroe" sounded just right for a star.

°office that chooses actors for parts in a film

°full of light, glowing

°immediately

But stardom was still far away. Marilyn's studio ignored her entirely and even dropped her at the end of the year. It was not a total loss for her because she had been given her first and badly needed acting lessons, and like all starlets she had posed for a multitude° of cheesecake photos.° It made no difference whether she wore a bathing suit or a potato sack—she always looked lovely. It was not just luck and nature; she was working at her beauty with complete dedication. She experimented endlessly with cosmetics and hair styles; she exercised and studied anatomy books. Her hair was bleached,° her hairline modified, her teeth straightened. Later she had her facial muscles tightened and her chin and the tip of her nose remodeled. She did not look as striking° in the flesh as she did on the screen, and without make-up she was not always recognized. But she could not go unnoticed when she moved. In one of her first pictures, in which she played Groucho Marx's secretary, she was supposed to walk away from him saying, "I don't understand why men follow me." Groucho watched her leave the set with amused appreciation. "That's a fine walk," he grinned° afterward. "Now do it again, only more so." Marilyn was too smart not to follow his advice. Her sexy, swinging walk was to remain one of her trademarks,° like her breathless whisper and tight dresses.

°very large number / °pictures showing the legs and figure

°artificially lightened

°very remarkable

°smiled broadly

°distinctive characteristics

The first three years of Marilyn's career did not bring her more than a few bit parts.° She kept herself alive by modeling. It was an uncertain, often sordid, life, full of humiliations that left a mark on her. Her memories never let her feel like a star even after she had reached the top. In 1949 she posed nude° for some "art" calendars that would not shock anybody today but that made a sensation when they were "discovered" after her first successes. If her studio and her agent were embarrassed by the scandal, Marilyn was not in the least. She fully appreciated its publicity value; moreover she had always liked to display her body. It was the only thing of which she was never ashamed or unsure. Naked, she felt admired, triumphant. She never buried herself in clothes; her dresses were low-cut and revealing, and she had them sewn on her to fit like a second skin.

In 1950 Marilyn attracted attention in a small part in *The Asphalt Jungle,* which had been obtained for her by a powerful protector. She had acquired several helpful friends by that time. One of them was Natasha Lytess, acting instructor of Columbia Pictures, who had trained Marilyn for a role in 1948, and who had since devoted considerable time and energy to teaching her how to act, think, and live. The relationship lasted until 1955, when Marilyn dismissed Natasha. But until then she never appeared in front of a camera unless Natasha was sitting behind it, approving or disapproving every word and gesture. Needless to say, the arrangement drove directors and other actors to distraction.°

Another protector, and the most influential by far, was the agent Johnny Hyde. Hyde was a powerful man in Hollywood when he met Marilyn and fell in love with her in 1950. He could not persuade her to marry him, but until he died of a heart attack at the end of that year, he fought to establish her as an actress and to convince producers and directors that she had the makings of a superstar. He was too wise to claim that she had talent; instead, he insisted that such personality did not need to be talented. He succeeded in getting her a part in *All about Eve,* a film that was to prove lucky for all its actors. Since she was appearing at the same time in *All about Eve* and *The Asphalt Jungle,* Fox was impressed enough to offer her a seven-year contract. The fan mail started piling up. The Hollywood columnists° included the new blonde in their gossip columns.° Soon *Life* and *Look* magazines were honoring

very small parts

naked, without clothes

drove . . . confused and disturbed

journalists

regular informal articles

her with long articles, and one critic ventured to declare her "a forceful actress." The studio, after having her co-star in several pictures, finally gave her a starring role in *Niagara* in 1953.

George Sanders, who acted with Marilyn in *All about Eve*, left a portrait of her in his book *Memoirs of a Professional Cad.°* "In her presence," he wrote, "it was difficult to con- ungentlemanly person
centrate. Her conversation had unexpected depths. She showed an interest in intellectual subjects which was, to say the least, disconcerting.° She was very beautiful and very inquiring and surprising, confusing
very unsure. As far as I can recall, she was humble, punctual° on time
and sweet. She wanted people to like her."

The question of Marilyn's intelligence and intellectualism° interest in mental and cultural things
has been the source of countless jokes. Many people, beginning with her studio's heads, always refused to see in her more than a dumb blonde with a star's usual pretense of cultural interest. Everyone laughed when the rumor spread that she was interested in the part of Grushenka in the film version of *The Brothers Karamazov;* everyone, that is, except her drama teachers and one of her directors, who protested that she would make a better Grushenka than any other actress they could think of. "I have a great advantage over those who ridicule me," remarked Marilyn, half hurt, half amused. "I have read the book!"

There is no question that Marilyn read a great deal, possibly because it was another way of improving herself. But even as a child she had always been genuinely° interested in reading of really, honestly
all kinds, and when she was still a starlet she had opened her first charge account, not at a dress shop, but at a large bookstore. Her friends never doubted her ability to appreciate what she read, although less sympathetic witnesses of her efforts swear that she could not understand most words. Such a close friend as the poet Carl Sandburg, and even Arthur Miller himself, who were good judges in the matter, found her intelligent, witty, and intuitive. She was certainly intelligent enough to admit frankly her ignorance of many subjects, and first of all of her own trade—acting.

III

Marilyn worked at her craft just as she had worked at her face. While she was a starlet she took acting lessons at Anton

Marilyn Monroe during shooting of The Seven Year Itch, *1954.*

Chekhov's[1] studio in Hollywood, and from 1955 until her death she worked in New York with the famous teachers Lee and Paula Strasberg. All three of them thought that she could become a great dramatic actress. After seeing her rehearse the part of Cordelia in *King Lear,* Chekhov had cried angrily, "They don't know what they are doing to you!" "They" were, of course, the filmmakers, who did not have the same glorious idea of Marilyn's talent. Chekhov maintained° that they did not   stated strongly
understand her; and Marilyn, who had gained some self-confidence with her stardom, was trying hard to believe him. But it is far from certain that she had the makings of a great actress even if she had been able to overcome her fear. Acting was a frightening experience for her, and she frequently suffered

[1]A nephew of the famous Russian writer Anton Chekhov.

from nausea, fainting spells, or skin problems when she had to face the cameras. Every film became an agony° worse than the preceding one. In spite of Chekhov's claim, Marilyn never did well in dramatic roles. But her work in *Gentlemen Prefer Blondes, How to Marry a Millionaire,* and *There's No Business like Show Business* proved that she could at least be an appealing comedienne. The critics always remained divided about her ability. Some found her "vapid"° or "vulgar, vaguely repulsive." Other were impressed by her beauty: "She could almost glow in the dark!" The most perceptive wondered. "She looks drugged," wrote an English columnist. "For all the wolf calls° that she gets and deserves there is something mournful° about Miss Monroe. She does not look happy." — deep suffering — empty — admiring whistles/very sad

She was not happy. Certainly, she had become Fox's biggest moneymaker. She had a tremendous popular following—five thousand fan letters a week. Whenever she appeared she was cornered by excited admirers and photographers. But there was no private happiness behind the facade,° and even her fame was not of the kind she would have liked. It was bitter enough to be playing dumb blondes forever, without being treated like one, especially by her own studio bosses. She was hurt by the amused contempt that she felt in the film colony, where she had no real friends. She resented her shallow roles; she resented the fact that she had no voice in the choice of her scripts and that her old contract was keeping her salary ridiculously low for a star. Hurt, she retaliated° as best she could. She arrived late on the set, unprepared and obviously indifferent to the hardships she was imposing on the other actors and the technicians. Scenes had to be redone forty or fifty times because she could not remember a four-word sentence. If something displeased her, she locked herself in her dressing room, or failed to show up at all for days. Her behavior disgusted the people who were forced to work with her; but her fans loved the radiant° child-woman on the screen and sympathized with her for what they had read about her youth. They became wildly enthusiastic when, in January 1954, she married another popular star, baseball hero Joe di Maggio. — outward appearance — got even — luminous, brilliant

By September the marriage was over. Both Joe and Marilyn had found it difficult to adjust to the other's established way of life. Above all, di Maggio, who was a conservative man, objected strongly to the extraordinary and often demeaning° demands of a sex-queen's career. He wanted her to quit. Her — lowering in dignity clothes, her roles, her publicity offended him. Even their honeymoon° had left something to be desired. Marilyn had flown to Korea to cheer the troops, while Joe was promoting baseball in Japan. She caught pneumonia singing in the snow in flimsy° dresses, but she was delighted with the trip. Afterward, she always claimed that it had been the high point of her life. And perhaps it was, not so much because of the adulation of the soldiers but because she had felt, for once, needed and useful.

wedding trip

very thin

The beginning of 1955 found her divorced from di Maggio and from Fox. She proclaimed herself independent, dropped her agent, dropped her lawyers, dropped Natasha, and with photographer Milton Greene formed a company called Marilyn Monroe Productions. The new company promptly bought the rights to a play by Terence Rattigan, *The Sleeping Prince,* and asked Sir Laurence Olivier to direct the film and play the male lead.° There was much laughter again, but, to everyone's surprise, Olivier accepted. Marilyn left Hollywood, head high and announcing her intention to start a serious career. But she had not reached happiness yet. She had started drinking too much, taking too many pills, and, like her mother, she was alternating between depression and wild rages. In New York, though, she did work hard at Strasberg's studio, and she was making plans for her future. She also renewed acquaintance with the man that she most wanted to see on the East Coast—playwright Arthur Miller. Miller had made a huge impression on her when they had met in Hollywood in 1950. "It was just like running into a tree, you know?" she had said. Miller was attracted too, but in 1950 he had been a married man. Now that he was divorcing his wife, the romance went like wildfire.°

main actor's part

at tremendous speed

Although considered one of the major American playwrights of the period, Miller was also a controversial° figure because it was known that he had been interested in communism. In the spring of 1956, when he and Marilyn were about to be married, he was requested by the House Un-American Activities Committee to give the names of the intellectuals he had seen attending communist meetings. He refused to name them, and for a while it looked as though the bridegroom° would spend his honeymoon in jail. Fortunately, the committee responded to public protest by dismissing the case, and Miller was allowed to accompany his wife to

causing arguments

newly married man

England, where Olivier was waiting to start *The Sleeping Prince*—renamed *The Prince and the Showgirl.* Lee and Paula Strasberg went with them; Paula was now taking the place of Natasha behind the cameras.

Marilyn regarded Miller with more than love; she was in awe° of him. She loved his children; she loved his parents, particularly his father, Isidore Miller, who returned her affection and would remain her loyal friend to the end of her life. For the first time Marilyn felt that she had found security. She wanted to have children of her own; she even underwent surgery to have a better chance of being a mother, but that dream never came true. Still, with an admiring husband by her side and a family behind her, she felt that she had become a valuable person and even, possibly, an actress.

Almost from the first day, however, the filming of *The Prince* was an ordeal° for all involved. Marilyn's peculiar way of acting shocked Olivier, who further resented her conferences with Paula. Conscious of being inadequate,° Marilyn suspected Olivier of looking down on her. She became nervous and difficult; she failed to show up on the set; she drank, raged, forgot her lines, and fought her chronic insomnia° with heavy doses of Nembutal, which left her groggy° and sick during the day. The job of keeping her reasonably sober and working fell on Miller. Soon she started suspecting him. He too, she thought, was disapproving of her; he too was betraying her. When they finally returned to the United States, the marriage was already showing signs of strain.

From then on things went steadily from bad to worse. Marilyn, who had dropped her partner Milton Greene abruptly, agreed to make three films for Twentieth-Century Fox besides those she was planning to make for her own company. The first one was *Some Like It Hot,* under the direction of Billy Wilder, who barely survived the experience. Arthur Miller had to fight the same battle all over again against a Marilyn increasingly suspicious, bitter, and abusive.° Miller was exhausted, disturbed, and certainly unhappy to find that his duties as nursemaid and impresario° had stopped his own work entirely. In the five years of their marriage, he wrote only a few short stories, some inspired by his wife. Those he collected into a film script that he entitled, fittingly, *The Misfits.*

After *Some Like It Hot* Marilyn made *Let's Make Love,* a disaster as a film and a private failure for her as well. She fell in

awe° fearful admiration

terrible experience

not good enough

inability to sleep

confused, in a stupor

insulting

theatrical manager

love with her co-star Yves Montand, who made it clear that he had no intention of leaving his wife Simone Signoret for her, even if Miller was past caring. When the Millers started filming *The Misfits* with Clark Gable in 1960, they were barely on speaking terms. The work was a nightmare. At one point, Marilyn fell so ill that her director sent her to a clinic for repairs. Strangely enough, when it was all done, *The Misfits* turned out to be one of her best films, and Marilyn looked very beautiful and very moving. But the film was just finished when Clark Gable died of a heart attack, and the Miller marriage fell apart. The divorce became final in 1961, and Miller remarried that same year.

Marilyn drifted back to the West Coast, putting up a brave front of shrill° gaiety. She bought a house and went to Mexico to chose the furnishings herself. Miller's father and some friends—Frank Sinatra, Dean Martin, the Strasbergs, and, most of all, Joe di Maggio—remained in close touch with her. Their affection and the care given by her various attendants helped her during the day, but they could not carry her through the sleepless nights. Neither another stay in a clinic nor visits to a psychoanalyst° seemed to help much. She tried, nevertheless, to get interested in *Something's Got to Give,* a vapid film for Twentieth-Century Fox. Drugged and lost, she was not likely to behave better on the set than she had before. She showed up so irregularly and made such impossible demands that the studio executives finally fired her in June 1962. It was a terrible blow for Marilyn, who was engaged in another depressing affair with a married man and who felt again unwanted as a woman and as an actress.

She had made many attempts at suicide before. But it does not seem that she intended to kill herself that Saturday, August 5, 1962. When she retired for the night she had plans for the next day, and she chatted by telephone with several friends, including Di Maggio's son, for whom she had great affection. When she started to feel the effect of the overdose she must have tried to reach her masseur,° whose answering service recorded her last call. Early in the morning her housekeeper found her dead, still holding the receiver.

The world was shocked. People blamed themselves and each other. But was anybody in particular responsible? Who could have cured Marilyn and saved her simultaneously° from the contempt she had for herself and from her ruthless ambition?

°high and sharp

°one who treats mental problems

°man trained to rub the muscles

°at the same time

Marilyn Monroe

So many people had failed her, patronized or ridiculed her, that she could not take herself seriously. A successful marriage might have helped, but none of hers ever worked. She could not even have a child. She tried to compensate° by attempting   make up
to become a "serious" actress, who would be admired and respected. But she was only a comedienne with a radiant presence and a sort of daffy° charm. She wanted more, and, in   silly, funny
the words of one of her biographers, "she broke her heart trying to achieve something she did not have in her to accomplish." She is now a lovely, enduring memory. Her acting, her films, and her misery are now given more attention than they received when she was the sex symbol of the day. Only now does Billy Wilder, who could not bear to hear her name after their last ordeal together, say: "We miss her like the devil! A whole category of films has been lost with her gone. The luminosity of that face! We'll never replace her."

Questions

1. In what way is Marilyn Monroe remarkable among sex queens?
2. What did Arthur Miller do that was considered in bad taste?
3. Why is it obvious that Marilyn was not simple?
4. Since Billy Wilder did not like her, why did he find it worthwhile to make films with her?
5. Why should journalists have doubted what she was telling them about her childhood?
6. What kind of childhood did she have?
7. What happened to her after her mother's hospitalization?
8. What effect did the events of her childhood have on her character?
9. What does her desire to become a Christian Scientist and later a Jew reveal about her character?
10. How did she happen to become a model?

Vocabulary

A   *Fill the blanks with an appropriate word taken from the list.*

matinee	mediocre
brutal	smother
insecure	myth
mischievous	conflicting
fabulous	tragic
rape	cope

1. The film inspired by Marilyn's life was neither good nor bad, it was _____.
2. Marilyn's grandmother had tried to _____ her under a pillow.
3. She had no confidence at all; she felt very _____.
4. Not everyone can handle fame; Marilyn could never _____ with hers.
5. People never agreed about her; they had _____ opinions.
6. Her grandparents and her mother suffered from paranoid schizophrenia; it was a _____ family history.

B   *Choose the most accurate of the three statements.*

1. A myth is
   a) a small butterfly
   b) an unreal being or story
   c) a sad play

2. A martyr is
   a) a person who has suffered for a cause
   b) the circle of light around a saint's head
   c) an idea

3. A tomboy is
   a) a girl
   b) a boy
   c) a symbol

4. To foresee an event is
   a) to be afraid of it
   b) to change it
   c) to see it in advance

5. A tart is
   a) a woman of limited intelligence
   b) an actress of limited talent
   c) a woman of limited virtue

6. A candid opinion is
   a) a stupid opinion
   b) a frank opinion
   c) a favorable opinion

Structures

A   *Following the example, combine the two sentences of each pair, using* **by** *and a gerund.*

Example   They told her that she was not a member of the family. They made her unhappy.
They made her unhappy **by telling** her that she was not a member of the family.

1. She talked with the tenant. So she learned a great deal about moviemaking.
2. She became a Christian Scientist. She tried to please Ana.
3. Her father refused to meet her. He hurt her deeply.
4. They cut her pictures out of the books. They show their admiration for Marilyn.

5. They could have treated her with respect. They would have made her very happy.
6. She told interesting stories about her youth. So she became popular with the newsmen.

B **Example** She dreamed of acting.
It is not surprising that she should have dreamed of acting.

1. She attracted the boys.
2. She became a loner.
3. Marilyn felt unwanted.
4. Billy Wilder was mad at her.
5. She kept a bad memory of her childhood.
6. People did not understand her.

Topics for Discussion or Written Assignment

1. Have you ever seen Marilyn Monroe on the screen or on television? What did you think of the film? Of her acting? Do you understand why she became a star?
2. In his play *After the Fall,* Arthur Miller patterned the characters after himself and after his successive wives, mixing fact and fiction. "Maggie," in whom everyone recognized Marilyn Monroe, emerges as a pathetic, rather unappealing person. Should or shouldn't the writer have used such a famous person (who was also his own wife) in his play? Do you think that an author can take his inspiration wherever he finds it? Should he make sure that the model cannot be recognized, or "sweeten" the facts, or do as he pleases without any limitation?
3. What is a sex queen? What names come to your mind? What do you think of sex queens and of the amount of attention paid to them? Do you think that Marilyn Monroe would have such a successful career nowadays, or is that type of actress a thing of the past?

Exercises for Section II *pp. 23-26*

Questions

1. Why can it be said that it was helpful for Marilyn to look so lost?
2. Some people had a severe opinion of her. What did they say?
3. What does her first divorce suggest about her?
4. Was her first year at Twentieth-Century Fox a total loss? Why?

5. Would you describe her beauty as entirely natural? Why?
6. What were her assets, useful qualities, and gifts?
7. Why did she like to show her body?
8. What was the importance of Natasha Lytess in the making of Marilyn's career?
9. What impression did George Sanders have of Marilyn?
10. Do you think that Marilyn sincerely enjoyed literature? Why?

Vocabulary

A 1. A _____ is a flesh-eating fish.
2. Starlets often sit for _____ photos.
3. The _____ department chooses the actors for the parts in a film.
4. A person who is always on time is _____ .
5. A gossip _____ writes about starlets and stars.
6. Marilyn's whisper, tight dresses, and sexy walk were her _____ .

B *Repeat the following sentences, replacing the word or phrase in italics with one with similar meaning taken from the list. (Make necessary adjustments for the tense of verbs.)*

sordid	genuinely
endlessly	luminous
inquiring	bleach
disconcerting	dismiss
striking	forthwith
venture	furthermore

1. She was accepted *immediately* among the Fox starlets.
2. She was a woman of *very remarkable* beauty.
3. She was *honestly* interested in books.
4. She had a *glowing* skin.
5. Her interest in intellectual subjects was *confusing*.
6. She *sent away* many people who had helped her.

Structures

A **Example** She felt vague about life, but not about her career.
However vague she may have felt about life, **she did not feel vague** about her career.

1. She was shy, but not too shy to present herself to Ben Lyons.
2. Zanuck was impressed, but not enough to give her a role.

3. She was pretty, but not as pretty as she looked on the screen.
4. She was unsure of her talent, but not unsure of her body.
5. He was powerful, but not enough to get her a starring role.
6. She was good, but not good enough to play Grushenka.

B **Example** He had not foreseen that she would be a photographer's dream.
What he had not foreseen was that she would be a photographer's dream.

1. Jim did not know that she wanted to be an actress.
2. I had never heard that she was punctual.
3. Johnny Hyde was hoping that she would marry him.
4. He always said that she did not need talent.
5. Natasha taught her to think and to live.
6. He wanted to establish her as an actress.
7. She needed to make money.
8. Groucho told her to keep her sexy walk.

Topics for Discussion or Written Assignment

1. Do you think that the discovery that a star posed nude for a calendar or a magazine would create a scandal today? Would it help or hurt the star's career? What helps an actor's career? Can anything hurt it nowadays? The gossip columnists of the 1950s considered themselves the makers and breakers of stars; were they right?
2. Johnny Hyde thought that Marilyn had the makings of a superstar. What do you think of his opinion? What *are* the makings of a superstar?
3. What is the difference between an actress and a star? Give examples.

Exercises for Section III pp. 26-32

Questions

1. Why was Anton Chekhov so angry at the filmmakers who had been using Marilyn?
2. How did Marilyn feel about acting?
3. Why wasn't she pleased with her career?
4. How did she show her resentment at the studio?
5. Why was she so pleased with her trip to Korea?
6. Why did the filming of *The Prince and the Showgirl* strain Marilyn's marriage to Arthur Miller?
7. What effect did his marriage to Marilyn have on Arthur Miller's work?
8. What depressing events happened to Marilyn before her death?

9. What caused her death?
10. What did her biographer mean when he wrote, "She broke her heart trying to achieve something she did not have in her to accomplish"?

Vocabulary

A   *Repeat the following sentences, replacing the word or phrase in italics with one with similar meaning taken from the list.*

undergo	ordeal
claim	perceptive
vapid	retaliate
groggy	nausea
compensate	inadequate
shrill	mournful
shallow	insomnia

1. The filming of *The Prince and the Showgirl* was a *severe experience* for all involved.
2. Marilyn felt, with good reasons, that she was *not good enough.*
3. She also suffered from her chronic *inability to sleep.*
4. She took drugs that left her *confused* during the day.
5. One English columnist had written that there was something *very sad* about her.
6. Since she thought that her husband had betrayed her she wanted *to pay him back.*
7. Her laughter sounded *high and sharp.*
8. Her fame as a sex queen did not *make up* for the failure of her private life.

B   *Fill the blank in each of the following sentences with a noun suggested by the verb.*

1. **fail**   Marilyn was deeply hurt by the _____ of her marriage to di Maggio.
2. **convince**   Chekhov made her share his _____ that she could be a great actress.
3. **intend**   Yves Montand had no _____ of leaving his wife.
4. **advise**   Marilyn needed Paula's _____ about every scene, every move.
5. **refuse**   The actors and the crew resented her _____ to show up on the set.
6. **contradict**   From the _____ in the judgments of those who knew her it is obvious that she was not simple.
7. **deepen**   Her conversation had unexpected _____ .
8. **warm**   To her friends, she only showed kindness and _____ .

Structures

A *Combine the two sentences of each pair, using the conjunction* **after** *as in the example.*

Example Chekhov saw her rehearse the part of Cordelia. He cried that the film directors did not understand her talent.
After seeing her rehearse the part of Cordelia, Chekhov cried that the film directors did not understand her talent.

1. Marilyn finished *Gentlemen Prefer Blondes*. She was immediately cast in another comedy.
2. A famous critic watched her in five of her films. He wrote that he found her vulgar and vaguely repulsive.
3. Marilyn read his article. She declared angrily that he had no taste at all.
4. Olivier explained to her what he wanted her to do. He had to wait while she asked Paula's opinion.
5. Frank Sinatra heard that she was alone and sick. He sent her a dog.
6. The housekeeper found her bedroom door locked. She decided to call the police.
7. Clark Gable finished filming *The Misfits*. He died of a heart attack.
8. Billy Wilder declared that she was the meanest woman in Hollywood. He added that nobody could replace her.

B *Repeat the following sentences, filling the blank with* **as** *or* **like**. *Remember that* **like**, *a preposition, introduces a prepositional phrase (Marilyn was beautiful like her mother and her grandmother).* **As** *introduces a subordinate clause (Marilyn was beautiful, as her mother had hoped she would be).*

1. Marilyn Monroe is not ridiculed now, _____ she used to be.
2. Some people even see her with a halo, _____ a saint.
3. She was never considered a serious actress _____ Greta Garbo.
4. But on the screen she looked fabulous, _____ Garbo did.
5. Wilder said that, _____ many other stars, she was difficult.
6. She played baseball _____ a boy, but never looked _____ one.
7. Arthur Miller presented Marilyn _____ he remembered her.
8. Marilyn wanted to play with great actors _____ Laurence Olivier.

Topics for Discussion or Written Assignment

1. Marilyn considered herself a very unlucky woman. Do you agree?
2. How do you explain the interest that surrounds Marilyn Monroe today? Is it because of pity, admiration, nostalgia?
3. What does Marilyn's life reveal to us about Hollywood's star system and the importance of publicity and public relations?

Martin Luther King, Jr.

Malcolm X

Martin Luther King, Jr.
Born January 15, 1929
In Atlanta, Georgia
Died April 5, 1968

Malcolm X
Born May 19, 1925
In Omaha, Nebraska
Died February 21, 1965

"I don't know any Negro who doesn't really want the American Dream,"[1] says Carl Stokes, the black former mayor of Cleveland. "You take some of the most militant° Negroes in the United States; give them the things middle-class America enjoys, and they'll barely listen to anyone yelling 'Uhuru!' "° Not everybody would agree with him. Revolutionist Rap Brown would be likely to protest that he, for one, wants the destruction of the whole system; and Malcolm X used to sneer° that there was no American Dream, only an American Nightmare.° Nonetheless, those fortunate Negroes who do enjoy a measure of the Dream seem to find it to their taste, and they often annoy civil rights leaders by their lack of revolutionary spirit. It is all too clear that they would rather join the country club than blow up a police station or move to Nigeria. And one suspects that neither Rap Brown nor Malcolm X would have come to hate the American way of life if it had been possible for them to bear its imperfections in harmony and equality with the whites—if only they had been allowed to live with dignity.

Being accepted as human beings and full citizens has been the black Americans' goal for three and a half centuries. They have tried every conceivable approach. Some have used violence—there are riots now, as there were slave rebellions in the early days. One of them was led by Nat Turner, who has been brought back to the attention of the public by William Styron's best-selling book *The Confessions of Nat Turner.*

Some preferred to reason with the whites. In a letter to Thomas Jefferson, black mathematician Benjamin Banneker reminded the author of the Declaration of Independence that all men had been created equal and given the same right to life, liberty, and the pursuit of happiness. Why then, he wanted to know, was the new republic keeping so many men "in groaning captivity and cruel oppression?" At about the same time, some black Christians walked out of churches where they were forced to worship in segregated° sections. Their action did not seem to disturb the consciences of the white

favoring force and violence

"Independence" (Swahili)

say with contempt

bad dream

separated

---

[1] An idealized view of American society, prosperous and happy, with equal opportunity for all.

worshipers, but two prosperous free Negroes of Boston hit upon° a more effective line: they announced that they would not pay taxes as long as they were not permitted to vote. Whereupon Massachusetts promptly granted full voting rights to her Negro residents.

The cry for freedom was answered in 1865 by Abraham Lincoln's Emancipation Proclamation. But the former slaves soon realized that they had won only an illusion° of freedom. What good was being free if they could not support themselves,° either because of their lack of education or because the white population did not let them practice the skills they had? Far from disappearing with time, discrimination° worsened, particularly in the South, where special laws were passed to keep the blacks in fear and poverty. No Negro in his senses° would have ever tried to use a "white" drinking fountain or rest room; none would have dared enter a "white" restaurant, or demand to be addressed as "Mr. Smith" instead of "boy." Any attempt to register to vote was sure to bring threats, or worse; and a black man even looking in the direction of a white woman was simply asking to be lynched.° In the North, where segregation was not supported by law, it worked in more subtle° ways, but it came to the surface when large numbers of Negroes moved to the big industrial cities to seek work. They were gradually pushed into the most miserable parts of town, and there most of them still exist, crowded into slums,° cheated by landlords and merchants, and ready to listen to any leader who offers a way out.

The black cause has never lacked intelligent and dedicated spokesmen.° There have been "violent" and "nonviolent" ones; there have been those who talked of brotherhood and those who urged political action or a separate black culture. Frederick Douglass saw salvation in hard work and education. So did Booker T. Washington, who, being a practical man and a diplomat, sought to calm the fears of the whites. Abandoning all claims to social equality and to higher education, he fought for the establishment of trade schools in which Negroes could learn industrial and agricultural skills. His moderation angered his friend, scholar° W. E. B. Du Bois, who wanted to see a college-educated black elite° lead Negroes toward total equality with whites. In 1910, with a few concerned whites, Du Bois founded the National Association for the Advancement of Colored People (NAACP), an organization dedicated to the

Margin glosses:

found by chance

false appearance

to earn enough money to live on

prejudice against a particular group

with his reason

hanged by a mob

secretly active

dirty, overcrowded sections

speakers for a cause

highly educated man

highest class

pursuit of civil and political rights by legal means. From the very beginning some blacks refused to join the NAACP because of its mixed membership. More and more Negroes were determined to have nothing to do with the race that had debased° theirs and that had spawned° the Ku Klux Klan (in 1875).[2]

made low, vile/ gave birth to

In the early 1920s, a very big, very black Jamaican named Marcus M. Garvey appeared on the scene in flamboyant° robes and feathered hats and startled everyone by declaring that Black was Beautiful. Black people, he explained, had every right to feel proud of their blackness; they were members of a mighty race with a glorious history and, no doubt, a great future in their homeland. Back to Africa! Forget the whites! As a first step in the right direction, he acquired a steamship company, and tried to organize a mass emigration of blacks to Liberia, the new nation started in 1822 by a group of freed slaves on the west coast of Africa. The Liberian leaders, sympathetic at first, cooled visibly when it was rumored that Garvey was planning to take over the government of their country. It may not have been true at all, and anyway it is doubtful that the company's three rickety° vessels could have floated very far. But Garvey's ideas were sounder° than his fleet. He urged blacks to make themselves economically independent while waiting for the great migration. Many obeyed and started businesses, farms, and newspapers; millions joined Garvey's Universal Negro Improvement Association and dreamed with him. Unfortunately, he was jailed for using the mail to defraud° and shipped back to Jamaica in 1927. His "ministers," however, kept spreading his doctrine, and none did it with more devotion than Earl Little, a former Baptist preacher from Georgia who lived in Nebraska. For his activities Little was hounded by white racists,° forced to move to Illinois, and brutally murdered in 1931. The seventh of his eight children, Malcolm, was to make himself famous—or notorious°—under the name of Malcolm X.

ornate and colorful

falling apart
more healthy

stealing money by deception

believers in the superiority of their own race

famous but disapproved of

Today Malcolm X and Martin Luther King, Jr., stand high in the pantheon° of black leaders. Dr. King was enthroned there at the age of twenty-seven and has been worshiped ever since by a vast majority of black people. Most Negroes still consider him the most effective leader of the century. Malcolm X, feared as a

collection of gods (fig.)

[2]Secret organization of white racists aimed at terrorizing Negroes and denying them equality.

ghetto° rabble-rouser° in his lifetime, has only gained sainthood since his death. His following was much smaller than Dr. King's, but he is the model of the Black Panthers and of today's young militants, such as Rap Brown, Eldridge Cleaver, and Stokely Carmichael. Both Malcolm and King were brilliant men, blessed with that "star quality," that "charisma,"° that draws people and makes mountains so much easier to move. They had little else in common, except that they both yearned° to see their black brothers regain a place among men, along with their own self-respect. Malcolm always insisted that the most hateful crime of the whites had been to convince the blacks that they were indeed inferior, that the only acceptable standards in all things were the white standards. Both Malcolm and King had experienced the bias° for themselves. As a young man, Malcolm had gloried in his light complexion, and he had gone through tortures to "conk" (straighten) his hair. As for Martin, he had always done his best not to fit the stereotype° of the careless, loud, grinning Negro. He dressed severely, avoided smiling to the point of looking solemn, and never ate a watermelon in public if he could help it. As adults, both of them watched with joy young blacks expressing their racial pride through Afro hairstyles, African fashions, and Swahili greetings.

Beyond this, there was not much on which Reverend° King and the Muslim Malcolm could see eye to eye.° In attitude, in methods, and even in goals, they were opposites. King's dream was to see the black Americans smoothly integrated° with their white countrymen, all living, voting, and being educated together as brothers. They were brothers in his eyes; they were all God's children. The bad relations between them could surely be improved. All that was needed was patience and love, the "weapons" of Jesus, which had been successfully put to use by the non-Christian Gandhi when he wanted to free his India from the British.

Gandhi! Malcolm sneered. Gandhi had succeeded because he was a big black elephant sitting on a small white mouse; but King was a small black mouse on top of a big white elephant. He could not win. Integration was a bad joke, segregation an insult; the only good solution to the racial problem lay in the complete separation of the races, either through the return of the Negroes to Africa or through the creation of a black state in North America—if enough good land could be wrenched° from

Glossary:
- segregated slum/man who excites the masses
- quality that inspires enthusiasm and devotion
- desire strongly
- strong opinion
- fixed idea about a race or group
- title for a clergyman
- see . . . to agree
- brought together
- taken by force

the whites. The details of these operations tended to remain vague, but Malcolm's message rang clear: the whites were not worth winning over.° $\qquad$ gaining the good will of

This was not his own concept, but the creed° of his religion, a religious beliefs version of Islam presented by Elijah Muhammad of Chicago. Muhammad was teaching his small group (the Nation of Islam) that Allah was the only God and that he—Muhammad—was Allah's chosen prophet. At the beginning of time, the story went, Allah had created men, all of them black. It was only six thousand years ago that a demon° had spoiled the divine work evil spirit by bleaching some of God's men and producing strange white creatures. Eventually—and surely by foul means°—those had foul . . . evil methods taken over the world. They were not men at all; they were devils—wicked, unredeemable,° and, therefore, expendable.° impossible to save / unnecessary As a matter of fact, Allah was about to punish them for their evil deeds—in ten years or so.

In the meantime there was no point in trying to mix with them. Blacks were not to marry them or participate in any social or political event with them, not even to the extent of voting. There was no point in trying either to love them or to bear their savagery patiently. "There is nothing in the book of Islam, the Koran, that teaches us to suffer peacefully," said Malcolm X as a minister of the Nation of Islam. "Be peaceful, be courteous, obey the laws . . . but if anyone puts a hand on you send him to the cemetery. An eye for an eye, a life for a life!" For Christianity Malcolm had nothing but contempt. Christianity was a fraud,° and the black clergy had been the curse° of the deception/cause of harm black man, whom they had tamed and talked into waiting meekly for heavenly rewards.

II

The gulf° between Malcolm X's and Martin Luther King's wide separation points of view is easier to understand if one considers their backgrounds.° The son and grandson of respected Baptist past experience and surroundings ministers, Martin Luther King, Jr., belonged to a relatively — comfortable and secure family in Atlanta, Georgia. He had grown up happily—a bright and sensitive boy of thoughtful disposition. It is said that even in his youth he hated violence and never fought back when he was bullied° by older boys. His mistreated dislike for the use of force did not prevent him from becoming a first-class wrestler,[3] however. He was also a good tennis player and a fine athlete altogether.

Skipping° a grade here and there, Martin raced his way °*here, bypassing, omitting* through a succession of fine schools, topped by the Crozier Theological Seminary in Pennsylvania, Harvard, and Boston University, from which he received a Ph.D. in systematic theology[4] in 1955. While studying in the North, the young Southerner was pleasantly surprised to find that he could associate with white students, and that he was admitted without trouble to any restaurant or theater in town. That would not have been possible in the South, not even in "liberal" Atlanta. "The wholesome° relation we had," he °*healthy, good* related later, "convinced me that we have many white persons as allies. . . . I had been ready to resent the whole white race, but as I got to see more of the whites, my resentment was softened and a spirit of cooperation took its place." Malcolm X would not experience that feeling until 1964, one year before his death.

Although happily immersed° in his studies, Martin never let °*deep* philosophy ruin his chances with pretty girls. He seemed to find them all attractive, and most of them seemed willing to return his feeling. But in 1953 he met his match in a spirited young woman from Alabama, Coretta Scott, who was studying voice at the Boston Conservatory of Music. Coretta was planning a singing career. She had no use for Southern Baptist preachers, and the last thing she wanted to do was to marry one. But Martin made skillful use of his eloquence and of his mellow° baritone,° and marry they did. In September °*soft and rich/ deep male voice* 1954, the Reverend Martin Luther King, Jr., and his bride moved to Montgomery, Alabama, and the minister took charge of the Dexter Avenue Baptist Church. Three months earlier Malcolm X had been appointed minister of Muslim Temple Number 7, in Harlem. He had not reached his pulpit° °*preacher's stand or desk* through a theological seminary.

Malcolm Little was born in Omaha, Nebraska. At the age of six he had seen his home burned down by white racists while white firemen looked on. He was eight when white men crushed his father's head and threw him on the streetcar tracks. His uncles had all died violently, one of them lynched. Young Malcolm watched his mother struggle to feed her family, but as

[3] A sport in which each of two men tries to force the other to the ground.
[4] Study of different religious systems and notions of God.

a Negro and Earl Little's widow, she could not find work. The little boy watched the white welfare° people bully and humiliate her, and finally lock her in a mental institution when she broke down. The children were put in foster homes. Malcolm landed in a good white family, but although he was well treated, it was rather as if he were a pet, and he noticed with mild surprise that even those kind people could not imagine that Negroes had feelings like their own. Malcolm accepted the small hurts just as he had come to accept being called "nigger" or "coon" by his classmates and his teachers. All Negroes were "coons"; it did not make any difference that he was the brightest student in the school, a star of the basketball team, and the president of his class. The really significant° blow came from the man he considered his best friend and adviser, his English teacher. It was the end of the school year, in seventh grade. The instructor asked Malcolm if he had given any thought to his future. "Yes," said the boy, "I'd like to be a lawyer." The teacher smiled: "Malcolm, you have got to be realistic about being a nigger. Lawyer—that's not a realistic goal for a nigger. You need to think of something you *can* be. Why don't you plan on carpentry?"

Malcolm never recovered. From cheerful and friendly he turned sullen° and touchy.° His puzzled foster parents finally agreed to let him go to live with his older sister in Michigan. In the black ghetto of Detroit, and soon in Harlem, young Malcolm launched into a new kind of life in the company of prostitutes, pimps,° drug dealers, addicts, gamblers, and racketeers of all kinds. He made a good living hustling° drugs, women, or whatever happened to bring the highest profit. In the process of guiding the whites who came to the ghetto to indulge in their vices, Malcolm developed a thorough contempt for the whole white race. There was nothing in his past to balance his judgment. In 1945, at twenty, Malcolm was arrested for armed burglary[5] and sentenced to ten years in jail.

For a whole year Malcolm ranted° and raged, "evil-tempered as a snake." The other inmates° called him Satan. Nothing and nobody frightened him in those days, but there was one man, an educated prisoner, who awed him. It was the first man whom Malcolm had ever seen "command total respect with words." Quietly, Malcolm began to borrow books, and he

[5]Forced entry into a house to commit robbery.

Margin glosses:
public relief organization
meaningful, important
silent and angry/ easily angered
man who protects and manages a prostitute
pushing, selling
spoke violently
prisoners

enrolled in correspondence courses in English and Latin. He was making fine progress when two of his brothers wrote him about the religion of Elijah Muhammad. Muhammad's creed had an enormous uplifting° value for the Negroes from the slums because it prodded° them into making themselves worthy of their divine father. It insisted that Allah's children had a right to stand tall, but only if they kept themselves clean morally as well as physically. They were forbidden to eat pork—the unclean meat—to dance, to date, to go to the movies, and to take long rests or vacations. Above all they were forbidden to have anything to do with the three poisons used by the white devils to debase them—alcohol, tobacco, and drugs.

°raising, improving
°pushed

Fascinated, Malcolm accepted the rules. He threw himself into an orgy° of education. He attended all available lectures and plowed his way through the large prison library. In history, anthropology,° religion, philosophy, he found everywhere "proof" of the arrogance° and dishonesty of the whites. Muhammad was encouraging him through letters. As soon as he was freed, in 1952, Malcolm rushed to Chicago to put himself at the prophet's service. It was at that time that he dropped the family name given to one of his ancestors by some "blue-eyed devil" and replaced it with the X symbolizing his forgotten African name. After watching his new disciple° for some time, Muhammad recognized the young man's exceptional ability and energy. He gave him positions of increasing responsibility in several of his temples and finally made him minister of Temple 7, in New York, in 1954.

°frenzy
°science of the development of humans
°excessive pride
°person who follows a teacher

Malcolm spread his message of hate with contagious° passion. Nothing else counted for him any more. His whole energy went into trying to enlarge the Nation of Islam and to find younger and more dynamic members. So far the strict Muslim code had struck most young blacks as too demanding. The membership remained small, but Malcolm had a tremendous effect on his audiences. In 1957 an encounter with the New York City police showed his hold on the black mob and on the disciplined "guards" of the Nation of Islam so clearly that a chief of police was heard to remark unhappily, "No one man should have that much power!" The police grew wary of him. The press became curious, and the public began to hear about Malcolm X and the Black Muslims. In 1959 Mike Wallace put together a television show entitled "The Hate that Hate

°spreading easily

Produced" about Malcolm and his nation. The show chilled° its
viewers, including the black ones. *made cold with fear*

In the South, things had been happening to the resigned
blacks, to the surprised whites, and to Reverend Martin Luther
King, Jr. It had begun on December 5, 1955, when a quiet black
woman named Rosa Parks refused to give her seat to a white
passenger in a Montgomery bus. Mrs. Parks had no desire to
start another civil war, but, as she explained later, she was tired
and her feet hurt. Such arrogant behavior was not tolerated in
Alabama. In the buses, the seating arrangement had been
established long ago: the whites in front, the blacks in the rear.
If there were not enough seats for all, the Negroes had to give
theirs up. While he was a student, King had once been forced to
give up his seat and to stand "in deep anger" through the
remaining ninety miles of his trip. Sitting or standing, the
black passengers were liable to° be bullied and insulted. They *susceptible to, open to*
could not even board the buses with the whites; after paying
their fares in front they had to get off again and reboard through
the back door. Sometimes when the conductor felt like having
fun, he would drive off in the middle of the operation, leaving
the black passengers in the street, minus their fare.

The situation had been borne for years in silent resentment,
but the news that shy Rosa Parks had been arrested and jailed
aroused the black community. The leading black businessmen
and clergymen—among them Martin Luther King—decided
that the time had come to do something. They asked the
Negroes to boycott° the buses for twenty-four hours, while they *avoid the use of*
would attempt to make the bus company promise courteous
service and the right for any passenger to keep his seat to his
destination. The company refused. But, to the black leaders'
extreme surprise, the Negroes of Montgomery followed the
boycott order to a man. Something might indeed be done. The
leaders organized themselves into the Montgomery Improvement Association and elected Dr. King to head it. For the 382
days of the boycott, despite threats, harassment,° vilifications,° *constant attacks/ verbal abuse, curses*
and the bombing of his house, King kept the movement going,
the car pools running, and the spirit of the participants high.
"My feets is tired but my soul is rested," said an ungrammatical
but delighted walker. Victory came in December 1956 in the
form of a Supreme Court decision declaring the segregated
seating policy in Alabama buses unconstitutional.

Martin Luther King, Jr., emerged from the battle a national

figure. "I am worried to death," he said. "A man who hits his peak at twenty-seven has a tough job ahead. People will be expecting me to pull rabbits out of the hat° for the rest of my life." The Southern Negroes certainly did. He had become the new Moses. Actually, King had not started the boycott, and he had not shown himself a particularly able organizer or negotiator.° But he had brought something more powerful and more necessary than administrative ability to the boycott. He had been the guiding force, the philosopher of the campaign. At the very beginning he had shaped the strategy:° "Our method must be that of persuasion, not of coercion.° Love must be our regulating ideal. . . . If you will protest courageously and yet with dignity and Christian love, the historians of the future will have to pause and say, 'There lived a great people, a black people, who injected new meaning and dignity into the veins of civilization.'" Nobody had ever spoken in that way to the janitors° and housemaids of Montgomery. They straightened their backs and gave their hearts to the young pastor who had proved to them that they had some human dignity after all, that they were able to act like men, and that together they wielded° some power.

pull . . . trick performed by magicians

one who tries to reach an agreement between two groups

plan

force

caretakers of buildings

exercised

It was exciting news. The effect was soon felt all over the South. Black communities that had never dared anything started agitating to desegregate their buses, their stores, and their public facilities. From North Carolina to Mississippi, students launched sit-in campaigns to desegregate lunch counters. Everywhere King was begged to bring the weight of his prestige,° to instruct the "troops" in nonviolent methods, to advise, and to encourage. And so he did, borrowing (as he said) "the spirit from Jesus and the technique from Gandhi." As often as not he ended up in jail. But being jailed became part of the strategy, as well as inducing° the authorities to make mass arrests and on occasion to arrest children.

high reputation

causing

In 1956 the sixty-odd° protest groups that had sprung up in the South had been combined into the Southern Christian Leadership Conference (SCLC), headed by Dr. King. The SCLC planned the actions and ran a training school for nonviolent fighters. Not all of the campaigns supported by King and the SCLC succeeded in their specific° aims, but they did attract attention to the inequalities of Southern life. Some demonstrations were bloody and heartbreaking. The young "freedom riders," black and white, who attempted to travel together by

between sixty and seventy

particular

bus through the South in 1960, for example, were beaten by angry mobs; some were killed.

III

In New York, Malcolm X laughed at the stupidity of singing "I love everybody in my heart"[6] to white savages swinging bricks, bicycle chains, and baseball bats. But King knew better; the "savages" were very useful. When he could chose the battleground himself, he selected places where the marchers could count on the overreaction° of the authorities. He knew the effect that could be produced on television audiences by the sight of water from high-pressure firehoses hurling° people against walls, or by police dogs biting men, women, and children. Public opinion was indeed aroused. And in the spring of 1963 President Kennedy sent to Congress an important civil rights bill that was to be passed after his death, in 1965.

°excessive reaction

°throwing violently

What was Martin Luther King's finest hour? Was it in August 1963 when 200,000 black and white nonviolent marchers gathered in Washington and listened to his speech ("I have a dream . . .") at the Lincoln Memorial? Was it when he visited Gandhi's tomb in India? Was it when *Time* magazine chose him as Man of the Year for 1963? Or more likely when he was awarded the Nobel Peace Prize in 1964? By then he had reached international stature. He could talk to the President and associate with the high and the mighty of the world. On his return from Oslo, where he had received his prize, eight thousand people honored him in New York. There was an elegant reception in Washington, and at a "King Banquet" in Atlanta, seventeen hundred whites and blacks from all walks of life sang "We Shall Overcome" together.

Still, it was not all roses. International heroes are liable to draw criticism and Martin Luther King received his share. To Malcolm X he was an "Uncle Tom."[7] Even in the South, irreverent° young blacks were beginning to call him "De Lawd."° He was too timid, some said. Others found him too bold. And why, others would ask, was he not in jail more often?

°disrespectful

°Southern pronunciation of "The Lord" (*iron.*)

[6]A line from the chorus of one of the songs sung by the nonviolent marchers.
[7]Stereotype of the servile Negro, meekly obeying his white masters; from a character in Harriet Beecher Stowe's novel *Uncle Tom's Cabin.*

Aerial view of the March on Washington for civil rights, August 28, 1963. Crowds are massed around the Lincoln Memorial.

Why was he making speeches in universities when he should have been suffering with his troops? There were mutterings° about his administration, his finances, his methods, and his private life. An increasing number of Negroes were getting impatient with the nonviolent approach. Stokely Carmichael, from the Student Non-violent Coordinating Committee, first talked of Black Power in front of King. And Black Power meant violence, or, at the very least, self-defense.

    If Martin Luther King, Jr., had reason to feel discouraged, Malcolm X had also fallen on unhappy times, although he now had the support of his wife, a devout° Muslim like himself.

grumblings, complaints

deeply religious

Malcolm, having waited so long for somebody and something to believe in, was doing his best to ignore the ugly rumors about Elijah Muhammad. The prophet, it seemed, had a regrettable tendency to father illegitimate children. In 1963 Malcolm had to admit to himself that it was true—his beloved master was not above human weaknesses. He tried to swallow his disappointment and what he regarded as a betrayal of the Muslim ethical code. But Elijah Muhammad, for his part, was also having second thoughts about his too-brilliant minister. The young man was attracting too much publicity. Besides, he did not seem as interested in religion now as he was in civil rights and political action. He had even asked permission to join in the battle raging in the South. This idea was offensive to Muhammad. Soon Malcolm became aware of a disparaging° disrespectful campaign against him among the Black Muslims. In November 1963, on a small pretext,° Muhammad suspended him from his false reason position and failed to cancel the suspension in the following / months.

Malcolm held a press conference in the spring of 1964 to announce that he was now on his own° and that soon he would on . . . his own master be launching a new movement. But before starting his Organization of Afro-American Unity, he took the time to make two trips that had a profound effect on his thinking. First he went to Mecca, the Holy City of the Moslems, and there he discovered that the true Islamic religion had little in common with Muhammad's ideas. It was not even a purely° black completely religion. In fact, what struck Malcolm most during his travels was the brotherhood among black, white, and yellow pilgrims,° those who go to worship in a holy place and the courtesy with which he was treated everywhere. Back in the United States, he announced to his followers that what he had called "white" until then was not a color but an attitude, and that he was now willing to work with any man of good will regardless of color.

His second trip took him to Cairo for the Pan-African Conference of August 1964, and afterward to the independent nations of Africa. All the Africans received him with great honors and listened eagerly to his description of black life in America. He persuaded them to bring the plight° of the bad condition American Negroes to the attention of the United Nations, but they did not act very effectively, and Malcolm, disappointed, turned to the organization of his group. He did not want it to be a religious movement but a politically oriented one aimed at gaining equality by any means. There had to be a revolution, he thought, and revolutions are not achieved without violence. He did not believe any more that black Americans should return to Africa. What they had to do was transform the American system into a true democracy, preferably of a socialistic character. In the meantime, Malcolm was ready to cooperate with any civil rights leader to bring about small improvements. In order to prove it, in January 1965, he went to Selma, Alabama, where Martin Luther King's demonstrators were struggling to have Negro citizens registered to vote. It had turned into a bloody affair, and Dr. King was in jail. Malcolm delivered a rousing° speech in praise of violence to an applauding crowd. Then, sitting by Coretta King, he explained to her that he was trying to help her husband. He told her the whites might be more willing to listen to Dr. King's reasonable voice if they understood what the alternative° could be.

inspiring, exciting

other possibility

Perhaps Malcolm's fire and King's quiet determination would have worked well together, but they did not have time to find out. Malcolm was an exhausted man, harassed by the lack of money and by the threats of Muhammad's followers. He was attacked several times, and his house was bombed. On February 21, 1965, as he was beginning to address an audience in Harlem he was felled by a volley of shots.° Although two of the three men convicted for his murder were Black Muslims, many of Malcolm's admirers still suspect the CIA[8] or some old enemies from Malcolm's ghetto days. Tens of thousands of people attended his funeral. "We misjudged the support that man had," wrote one of the reporters.

volley . . . number of shots all at once

The voter registration drive in Selma proved successful in the sense that it helped the passage of a Voting Rights Act in 1966, just as the Montgomery boycott had helped the first Civil Rights Act of 1956. It also showed dramatically the involvement of the liberal whites, as thousands of white clergymen and social workers poured into Alabama to face the local racists and the governor. But King was dismayed° to find many of his own followers inclined to violence. He was shaken when the blacks booed° him during his visit to the Watts ghetto, in Los Angeles, after the riots of August 1965. Anxious to reach the Northern Negroes and, if possible, to win them over to his nonviolent philosophy, he tried an all-out° campaign against

disturbed

made sounds of contempt

complete, total

[8]Central Intelligence Agency; the agency of the United States government engaged in secret activities.

the appalling° housing situation in the slums of Chicago. After `deeply disturbing`
months of marches, demonstrations, and violent fights with
white mobs, King could not obtain more than some vague
promises from the mayor and the Chicago Housing Authority.
He had not convinced the cynical° ghetto dwellers of the `doubting and ironic`
effectiveness° of his method. And he was in the process of `ability to achieve results`
losing the support of President Johnson and his administra-
tion—his firm allies° until then—by his strong and repeated `friendly helpers`
condemnation of the Vietnam War.

King unhappily watched the bloody riots of the mid-1960s.
He wanted very much to organize a Poor People's March on
Washington that would be "the last desperate demand to stave
off° the worst chaos, hatred, and violence any nation has ever `keep away, prevent`
encountered." But while he was putting the wheels in motion,
a garbage° collectors' strike started in Memphis, Tennessee, `things thrown away`
and King went there to lend them a hand.° On April 5, 1968, on `lend . . . help them`
the balcony of his motel, he was shot to death by a deranged° `mentally ill`
man, James Earl Ray, who may or may not have been a hired
killer.

What did Martin Luther King and Malcolm X accomplish?
King's struggle with the Southern segregationists certainly
helped along the laws on civil rights, voting rights, and fair
housing that were passed between 1956 and 1968. But, as he
said himself, "You cannot legislate morality." Legislation
alone is not sufficient if it is not implemented,° and the new `put to use`
laws are still not totally respected in the Deep South. Racism
has not disappeared; neither have the slums, although some
progress has been made in desegregating public places, in
opening jobs, and in integrating schools. But King's great hope
of touching white America's conscience has been only partially
fulfilled, and in places the blacks' demands and activities have
produced a damaging backlash.° `strong reaction against`

King's policy is now rejected by many blacks, particularly
the young militants, students, and intellectuals, who prefer to
take their inspiration from Malcolm X. "King was a figure of
the dignity period," says one of his former followers. He was
"the last prince of nonviolence," says another. Whatever
approach the blacks choose to take now, they owe much to both
Martin Luther King and Malcolm X. One in the rural,° religious `of the country`
South, the other in the angry ghettos of the North, they have
given their black brothers a new pride and a new confidence in
themselves. They have shown them that they are not only

human beings in their own country but that they are part of a huge section of humanity extending far outside the United States. And black Americans will never again be as they were before 1955, when the Reverend King began preaching love and dignity to the boycotters of Montgomery and when Malcolm X's voice started being heard in Harlem.

Questions

1. What attitudes of black Americans do Carl Stokes and Rap Brown represent?
2. What different approaches have the blacks used in the past to solve their problem?
3. Which great black leaders of the past can you name?
4. What do you remember about the foundation of the NAACP (founders, date, goals, membership)?
5. What seemed new and surprising in Marcus Garvey's view of the black race?
6. What link is there between Marcus Garvey and Malcolm X?
7. What was Martin Luther King's and Malcolm X's common goal?
8. Did Malcolm X have many followers?
9. Why is he important?
10. What was Martin Luther King's dream concerning black and white Americans?
11. Did Malcolm X share that dream?
12. What was Malcolm X's solution to the racial problem?
13. What was Elijah Muhammad's version of man's creation?
14. What did Malcolm X think of the role of the black Christian clergy?

Vocabulary

A   *In your own words, what is*

1. a scholar?
2. a militant?
3. a slum?
4. a stereotype?
5. a firebrand?
6. an elite?

B *Repeat the following sentences, replacing the word or phrase in italics with one with similar meaning taken from the list. Make the necessary adjustments for the verbs.*

sound	spawn
expendable	grant
defraud	foul
yearn	sneer
subtle	integrated
flamboyant	wrench

1. Malcolm X *said contemptuously* that there was no American Dream.
2. Marcus Garvey made a big impression with his *loudly colorful* clothes.
3. He had *healthy* ideas.
4. Muhammad said that the whites were *to be given up as unnecessary.*
5. He and Malcolm thought that some good land could be *taken by force* from the whites.
6. Malcolm *had a strong desire* to see the blacks regain their self-esteem.

Structures

A Example   Their goal has always been to be accepted as full citizens.
      Being accepted as full citizens has always been their goal.

1. It was a good idea to remind Thomas Jefferson that all men have been created equal.
2. It was an even better idea to refuse to pay taxes.
3. In the South, it was often dangerous to register to vote.
4. The most hateful crime of the whites had been to convince the Negroes that they were inferior.
5. For the young blacks, a way of expressing their pride was to wear an Afro hair style.
6. It was not as easy as it seemed to return to Africa.

B Example   When he was a child, he went to a segregated school.
      As a child he went to a segregated school.

1. Being a minister of Garvey, he was haunted by white racists.
2. When he was a slave, Frederick Douglass learned to read.
3. Being a scholar, Du Bois believed in higher education.
4. Being heirs to a glorious history, the blacks have a right to be proud, he said.

5. When he was an adult, Malcolm hated his light complexion.
6. Being a religious man, Martin Luther King saw all men as God's children.

Topics for Discussion or Written Assignment

1. Some people have said that the Negroes were happier and safer as slaves than most of them have been as free men ever since the Emancipation Proclamation. Do you think that it could be true? Do you think that this could justify slavery?
2. Are the blacks (and other minority members) free men? Are they full citizens?
3. Do you approve or disapprove of the Negroes who refused to join the NAACP because the membership was mixed? Why?

Exercises for Section II   *pp. 46-52*

Questions

1. What kind of family did Martin Luther King come from?
2. How did he feel about white people when he was at the university?
3. Did Malcolm X ever feel the same way?
4. What reasons did Malcolm have to dislike the whites?
5. How was Malcolm treated at school?
6. What happened with his English teacher?
7. What kind of life did Malcolm have in Harlem?
8. What made Muhammad's creed uplifting for the blacks in jail?
9. How did the bus boycott start in Montgomery?
10. Why did Martin Luther King make such an impression on the black people of Montgomery?

Vocabulary

A *Fill the blank with the appropriate word, chosen from the list.*

significant   mellow
arrogant   sullen
uplifting   immersed
pulpit   wholesome
chilled   background

1. Martin Luther King was the son and grandson of Baptist ministers of Atlanta, Georgia. Malcolm X came from a very different _____.

2. Martin Luther King had a very _____ baritone voice.

3. He was _____ in his studies of philosophy and theology.

4. Martin Luther King was pleased by the _____ relations between black and white students.

5. From being cheerful, young Malcolm became _____ .

6. The one _____ blow came from a man he liked very much.

B 1. What does a wrestler do?
2. a janitor?
3. a negotiator?
4. a person who boycotts the bus line?
5. a person involved in a burglary?
6. the Welfare Department?

C *Fill the blank with an adjective suggested by the verb or noun.*

1. **system** Martin Luther King received a degree in _____ theology.

2. **succeed** The campaigns supported by the SCLC were not always _____ .

3. **arrogance** Martin had been ready to see all whites as _____ enemies.

4. **conceive** In their long struggle the blacks have tried all _____ approaches.

5. **reality** The teacher advised Malcolm to chose a _____ goal.

6. **thought** As a boy, Martin showed a sensitive and _____ nature.

Structures

A **Example** Now he accepts being called insulting names.
He has come to accept being called insulting names.

1. Now he understands that many whites agree with him.
2. Now they admit that Negroes have feelings like their own.
3. Now she accepts the idea of marrying a preacher.
4. Now they recognize his ability.
5. Now he has changed his judgment of the white race.
6. Now he understands the power of words.

B **Example** They keep themselves clean; they want to be worthy of their father.
They keep themselves clean **so as to be** worthy of their father.

1. He studied hard; he wanted to be as well educated as his friend.
2. He studied anthropology; he wanted to know more about races.
3. His brothers wrote to him; they wanted to instruct him about Islam.
4. They boycotted the buses; they wanted to make the company change its policy.
5. They organized nonviolent demonstrations; they wanted to attract attention to the inequalities of Southern life.
6. He organized a school; he wanted to have well-trained nonviolent fighters.

Topics for Discussion or Written Assignment

1. Throughout the world many people have been discriminated against because of religion, race, sex, age, occupation, or some other reason. Describe those that you know of, and indicate what, if anything, was done to change the situation.
2. Some people think that jails do more harm than good and that the only result is hardened criminals; others feel that the prisoners' life is much too easy and that prisons should be made a great deal harder. There are also different opinions about the death penalty. Explain the reasons for and against these different points of view.
3. Compare the influence that their religion had on Malcolm X and Martin Luther King.

Questions

1. What kind of places did Dr. King choose for his nonviolent demonstrations? Why?
2. On what occasion did Dr. King make his famous statement, "I have a dream"?
3. Why did Dr. King go to Oslo?
4. What did people find to criticize about Dr. King?
5. How did Malcolm X criticize him?
6. What happened to Malcolm X's attitude toward Elijah Muhammad in 1963? Why?
7. What important discoveries did Malcolm X make in Mecca?
8. How was he killed?
9. Why did Dr. King make his campaign against the housing situation in Chicago?
10. Was he successful in any way?
11. In what way has Dr. King been successful?
12. How is Dr. King regarded now?

Vocabulary

A   *Chose the most accurate of the three words or phrases.*

1. A rural community is
   a) in town
   b) in the suburbs
   c) in the country

2. A specific order is
   a) precise
   b) vague
   c) severe

3. If you make a disparaging remark about somebody
   a) you express admiration
   b) you are asking about him or her
   c) you speak badly of that person

4. When you are hurling something
   a) you are throwing something
   b) you are borrowing something
   c) you are pulling something

5. If he staved off a disaster
   a) he foresaw it
   b) he started it
   c) he prevented it

6. A person's plight is
   a) his religious belief
   b) a threat he is making
   c) his bad situation

B *Repeat the following sentences, after filling the blank with the word from the list that best replaces the word in parentheses.*

irreverent	liable
converge	implemented
alternative	backlash
garbage	boycott
vilification	induced
cynical	appalling

1. Living conditions in the slums are _____ (horrifying).
2. Many people have no _____ (other possibility).
3. After living there for many years, they feel _____ (doubtful and ironical) about politicians' promises.
4. There are many laws but they are not all _____ (carried out).
5. Even in the SNCC, young black students talked of Martin Luther King in a(n) _____ (disrespectful) manner.
6. Too much violence and forced desegregation threatens to cause a _____ (strong reaction) among the whites.

Structures

A Example Benjamin Banneker wrote to Thomas Jefferson.
       It was Benjamin Banneker who wrote to Thomas Jefferson.

1. W. E. B. Du Bois founded the NAACP in 1910.
2. Marcus Garvey was the first to say that Black was Beautiful.
3. Rosa Parks indirectly started the bus boycott in Montgomery, Alabama.
4. An old black woman said, "My feets is tired but my soul is rested."
5. The blacks booed Dr. King when he was in Los Angeles.
6. Two Black Muslims shot Malcolm X to death.

B *Rearrange the following sentences in order to put the emphasis on the phrase in italics, as shown in the examples.*

Examples The boycott started *on December 6, 1955,* in Montgomery.
It was on December 6, 1955, that the boycott started in Montgomery.

The boycott started on December 6, 1955, *in Montgomery.*
It was in Montgomery that the boycott started on December 6, 1955.

1. *During his visit to Mecca,* in the spring of 1964, Malcolm X discovered that Islam is not a purely black religion.
2. During his visit to Mecca, *in the spring of 1964,* Malcolm X discovered that Islam is not a purely black religion.
3. During his visit to Mecca, in the spring of 1964, *Malcolm X* discovered that Islam is not a purely black religion.
4. *On April 4,* Dr. King went to Memphis to help a garbage collectors' strike.
5. On April 4, Dr. King went *to Memphis* to help a garbage collectors' strike.
6. On April 4, Dr. King went to Memphis *to help a garbage collectors' strike.*

Topics for Discussion or Written Assignment

1. "You cannot legislate morality," said Martin Luther King. What did he mean? Do you agree? Is legislation useless?
2. Compare the methods used by Malcolm X and Dr. King to try to achieve racial equality. Show the advantages and disadvantages of each and comment on the importance of the results each achieved.
3. Many ways and methods have been tried or offered to solve the racial problem. Describe the ideas you have heard and indicate the strengths and weaknesses of each.

Leonard
Bernstein

When Leonard Bernstein was about ten years old, his Aunt Clara moved to a smaller house, leaving with the Bernsteins the pieces of furniture that could not fit in her new home. Such an ordinary event would not have been expected to change the course of her nephew's life. But Leonard's life did change, for among Clara's discarded° treasures was an old-fashioned upright piano, an unremarkable instrument with which the boy fell instantly in love. He had never been exposed to music before. No one in the family was musically inclined.° Leonard's grandfather had been a rabbi[1] in Russia, and his father, Samuel, a successful businessman, was hoping that Lenny would become a rabbi too. That reasonable dream was shattered° by the arrival of Clara's piano. Young Leonard could not be kept away from it. He spent hours at the keyboard, experimenting with sounds and harmonies° and getting on everybody's nerves°—especially on his father's. According to Samuel Bernstein, musicians were lazy, no-good beggars, the sort of people who wander around and play the fiddle° in barns at country weddings. In short, they were the shame of respectable families. His only son a musician? Never! Many years later he was to ask, "And how was I supposed to know that he would become *Leonard Bernstein?*"

°left behind

°having a gift for music

°broken

°pleasant combinations of sounds

°getting on . . . . irritating

°violin

Bernstein is the most spectacular conductor ever produced by the United States. For glamour, for charisma, for plain crowd appeal, few public men would be able to compete with him. Even John F. Kennedy, a charismatic personality himself, remarked after a gala° that "Lenny" was the one man in the world against whom he would not want to run for political office. And it was wisely said. Bernstein would be a difficult opponent to beat° because he possesses all the qualities that make a winner. He has intelligence and wit. He has energy, ambition, and perseverance.° He has the right amount of self-confidence. He is very lucky. And, of course, he is enormously talented.

°*here,* special, elaborate performance

°defeat

°persistence, desire to finish

Everything seems to come easily to Leonard Bernstein. One can imagine him playing the piano with one hand, writing a poem with the other, singing a song, planning his next concert,

[1]Hebrew, "my teacher." The religious leader of a Jewish community.

answering the phone, and somehow beating his son at chess—all at once and without undue stress. It is not so, naturally. Like all serious artists, Bernstein works long, hard, and quietly. And nothing infuriates° him more than the critics' constant references to his "facility,"° even if they have good reason to praise or deplore° the quickness and capacity of his mind.

From the first, learning was easy to Lenny. No subject bored or defeated him at school, and he was interested in practically everything. He loved history, sports, literature, poetry, and games, and took foreign languages in stride.° He now commands several, including Hebrew. Since his father absolutely refused to let him study music, Leonard tried to teach himself on Clara's upright. There was no question in his mind that he *had* to be a musician; music was not a subject, it was life itself. He could not do without it. After a long battle, he offered to give up all pocket money° if he could take piano lessons, and Samuel gave in. From then on Leonard learned with shameful ease by playing all the scores° that he could borrow from the public library and the tunes he heard on the radio. "I don't think that there was such a thing as technical difficulties for him," says his former piano teacher. There was no such thing as a one-hour piano lesson either. He never had enough; he was never out of questions. He wanted to know all the music in the world.

At thirteen he composed a "terrible but very passionate"° concerto and discovered opera[2]—another considerable event in his life. He sat every day at the keyboard singing the works of Verdi, Puccini, and Bizet[3] at the top of his young tenor voice. During his summer vacations at Sharon, Massachusetts, Leonard produced his own "revised" version of Bizet's *Carmen* and of some of his other favorite operas and operettas. The audience was appreciative, and even Samuel could not help feeling proud of his son, although not to the point of changing his mind about a musical career. Lenny did not want to be a rabbi? All right. But he would have to take his place in the family business right after college.

Off to Harvard went Lenny. He immersed himself in literature and philosophy (which pleased his father), while majoring in music under the guidance of the American

° makes very angry

° ease

° regret deeply

° took . . . learned without difficulty

° pocket . . . money given to children by parents

° copy of music showing the notes to be played

° full of strong emotion

[2]Dramatic musical work in which the words are sung.
[3]Composers of famous nineteenth-century operas.

composer Walter Piston. At that time he also met another famous American composer, Aaron Copland, and Dimitri Mitropoulos, who was then the conductor of the Minneapolis Symphony Orchestra. Both were to remain his friends for life.

With his strong personality, Bernstein makes friends and enemies with equal facility. People like or dislike him almost on sight. "When Lenny enters a room," says his sister, "the temperature changes; everybody reacts to him one way or another." Irresistibly° charming when he wants to be, he can [in a fascinating way] also be arrogant and tactless. At the Curtis Institute of Music of Philadelphia after his graduation from Harvard, he irritated one of his fellow students so much that the young man actually attempted to shoot him. However, it is a proof of Bernstein's warmth and loyalty as a friend that he has never lost the affection of those who became close to him in his youth. Aaron Copland is still devoted to him after thirty years, and so is Bernstein's former piano teacher, who is still with him as his [guardian . . . one who watches over and protects] secretary, advisor, and guardian angel.°

When Lenny left Harvard, the dreaded° family job was still [much feared and disliked] hanging over his head like the sword of Damocles.[4] He was rescued just in time by Dimitri Mitropoulos, who helped him get a scholarship to the Curtis Institute. There he continued his study of piano and composition and attended the conducting classes of Fritz Reiner, director of the Pittsburgh Symphony Orchestra. It seems curious that Bernstein, now famous for his exuberant° style on the podium,° should have received his first [full of life/ raised platform] training from Reiner, who led his orchestra by barely moving the tip of his baton.° Bernstein moves *everything*. He sways, [stick used by the conductor] jumps, dances, sings, and grimaces.° He has been known to [makes faces] swing his baton in both hands like a baseball bat. Once the baton flew into the lap of a woman in the audience, and friends asked him why he did not chain it to his wrist. He did not find the joke amusing in the least.

If Leonard did not profit from Reiner's lessons in restrained° [disciplined, calm] conducting, which did not suit his personality, he again proved to be such a remarkable musician that Reiner, Copland, and Mitropoulos persuaded Serge Koussevitzsky, director of the Boston Symphony Orchestra, to admit him to his summer classes at the Berkshire Music Center in Tanglewood, Massachusetts. In no time at all, Koussevitzsky "adopted" the

[4]In Greek myth, Damocles was forced to sit at a banquet beneath a sword hung by a single hair.

brilliant young man. He made him his assistant for the following summer and meanwhile helped him find work in New York, in order to prove to Leonard's father that music could support a man. Although he was very busy adapting° scores for a musical firm and appearing in public as lecturer-pianist and accompanist whenever he could, Bernstein found time to compose. From that period date his first symphony, *Jeremiah,* and a group of songs entitled *I Hate Music.*

In the summer of 1943, again through Koussevitzsky, Bernstein met the musical director of the New York Philharmonic, Artur Rodzinski, who engaged him at once as assistant conductor for the season. What do assistant conductors do? Mainly, they have to be prepared to replace at short notice any conductor who cannot appear for a scheduled concert. They study the scores, attend the rehearsals, and perhaps pray that the Almighty send a case of measles to the regular conductor before the performance. It seldom happens. As a matter of fact, no replacement had been needed at the Philharmonic for fourteen years. But after Bernstein joined it, the miracle occurred twice in two months for the lucky young man.

In November 1943, the Sunday of a concert found guest conductor Bruno Walter in bed with the flu.° Bernstein was not feeling much better himself—he had a hangover.° The night before, mezzo-soprano Jennie Tourel had sung *I Hate Music* at a recital, and there had been a party afterward to celebrate the success of the singer and the songs. Bernstein had hardly slept. Nothing, however, could have made him miss his chance to conduct the Philharmonic. At three o'clock, the scared and tired assistant conductor mounted the podium and bowed to the disgruntled° audience, which had come to see Bruno Walter and did not appreciate the substitution. To make matters worse, the concert was being broadcast,° and several critics, alerted to the change of conductors, had come to observe him. Bernstein gave his all.° The orchestra, following him with rare good will, played beautifully, and the audience gave the young maestro° a standing ovation. As luck would have it, another conductor had to be replaced a few weeks later, and Leonard scored another triumph. This time he had made his mark for good, and his life, which had never been idle, took on a frantic tempo.° Besides his work with the Philharmonic, the scores to study, and the rehearsals, he had to find time for

adapting° simplifying or changing

flu.° influenza, an infectious virus disease

hangover.° headache and pains caused by too much alcohol

disgruntled° in very bad humor

broadcast,° sent by radio

all.° did his absolute best

maestro° Italian, master

tempo.° rhythm

Leonard Bernstein   71 the interviews and the social invitations. He had to conduct *Jeremiah* with other orchestras, write a ballet for dancer-choreographer° Jerome Robbins, and try to finish his other compositions. The more attention he received, the more annoyed Rodzinski felt about his assistant's extraordinary climb. He often showed his bad humor, and one day, in a sudden fit of anger, he grabbed the young man by the throat, bruising his neck a little and frightening him considerably. The manager of the orchestra advised Bernstein that it might be wise to keep himself out of sight for the rest of the season.

one who creates a ballet

II

It is not easy to stay out of sight when you are in demand everywhere. During the year 1944 Bernstein was very much in view. He conducted a total of eighty-nine concerts—an astonishing number for a conductor without an orchestra. Could he do anything wrong? Despite a severe review by music critic Virgil Thomson, *Jeremiah* won the Music Critics Award as the outstanding° work of the year. The ballet for Jerome Robbins, *Fancy Free,* was so well received that Bernstein expanded° it into a musical comedy—*On the Town*—that had a huge success on Broadway. The professionals were shocked to see a "serious" musician compose commercial music, and even the fatherly Koussevitzsky admonished° his protégé° about the strange turn that his career seemed to be taking.

remarkable

enlarged, made longer

warned / French, one protected by another

But the sale of the movie rights of the musical allowed Bernstein to accept an unpaid but exciting position—the direction of the New York City Center Orchestra. His first orchestra! For three years Bernstein made it thrive.° But he could not stay with it any longer; there were too many other things to do. He was making numerous guest appearances all over the United States, and he was often conducting orchestras abroad. He was advisor to the Israel Symphony, professor at the Berkshire Music Center, and then professor at Brandeis University as well. He replaced Fritz Reiner as the head of the Pittsburgh Symphony for a while. And through it all he was composing a second symphony (*Age of Anxiety*), another ballet (*Facsimile*), a one-act opera (*Trouble in Tahiti*), and various pieces of symphonic music.

grow strong, successful

At the end of a long tour abroad in 1953, he was about to

enjoy a well-earned rest in Italy when he was asked by the director of Milan's famous La Scala Opera to substitute for a sick man once more. This time, it was to conduct Cherubini's opera *Medea* with Maria Callas in the title role. Bernstein did not know *Medea,* and he had never met Callas. He only knew that the mere mention of her name made many a brave conductor shudder.° The more impossible the challenge seemed, the more irresistible° it became. In the five days he had before the performance he studied the enormous score and cut out some "dead" portions, including an aria for Callas in the second act. This was a dangerous operation, but Lenny so charmed the terrible soprano that she approved all his cuts, sang enthusiastically, and has remained his loyal friend ever since.

shake with fear
too interesting to be
refused

Since 1951 Leonard Bernstein has been married to Felicia Montealegre, a beautiful Chilean actress who, like him, suffers from an overabundance of gifts. She is a fine musician, a former student of the famous Chilean concert pianist Claudio Arrau. She paints and sculpts with talent when she finds the time, and she often appears as narrator° in musical works such as Honegger's *Joan of Arc* and Bernstein's *Kaddish* (his third symphony). She also handles two houses, three active teenage children, and a restless husband whose schedule must have her wondering at times whether she has not been caught in the path of a hurricane. Bernstein's acceptance of the directorship of the New York Philharmonic in 1953 has been attributed to her influence.

person telling the story

Bernstein was not entirely certain that he wanted a position as demanding as the direction of a major orchestra. He would have preferred to continue his teaching, to play piano in concerts more frequently, to write books, and to compose as much as he liked. But he did accept the directorship, and he kept it for twelve seasons—longer than any other conductor.

The Philharmonic's reputation was not extremely good in 1953. The old orchestra was losing its audience. Its main problem was the lack of discipline of its members, all excellent musicians, but temperamental and always ready to take advantage of a conductor who did not dominate them firmly enough. They enjoyed ignoring cues° or dropping a false note or two at the most effective moment. Bernstein, who is at the same time very sure and very unsure of himself, must have wondered how he would be accepted by these men who had

signals

Leonard Bernstein singing while conducting

known him when he was Rodzinski's assistant, who still called him "Lenny," and who were generally older than he was. It took only one season to show that Lenny's baton worked like a magic wand.[5] When he left the Philharmonic in 1969, amid° *in the middle of* tears, ovations,° and lavish° presents, it had been transformed *loud, enthusiastic applause/ very generous* into a superb, cohesive° ensemble,° a true musical family. *firmly joined / group*

What did it? Part of Bernstein's success must be attributed to his friendly, but firm, type of leadership and to his obvious concern for the happiness of his musicians. Another factor is

[5]Stick used by a fairy godmother to make fantastic transformations.

the pride and pleasure, for the performers, of being members of a highly appreciated orchestra under a highly praised conductor; of playing to full houses° during longer seasons; of going on tours abroad; of making numerous recordings; of appearing on television programs like the popular Omnibus Music Appreciation Series and the Young People's Concerts; and of enjoying a corresponding increase in their income. Moreover, they respected their leader's professional excellence. They had many opportunities to make this clear, as people always seemed curious to know what they found underneath the Bernstein glamour. Unanimously° they proclaimed that they had found a great musician with a perfect ear, a contagious sense of rhythm, and the rare ability to make the music as clear and fresh to the players as to the listeners.

full concert halls

of one opinion

What about the listeners? They sat up in surprise, at one of the first concerts, when the maestro ran from his podium to a piano, singing "Where, oh where have the peagreen freshmen° gone?" Bernstein then proceeded to explain how Charles Ives had worked that old college song into his Second Symphony, which was about to be performed. From then on the Thursday night concerts remained a sort of music appreciation class for adults, starting with a lecture in the casual Bernstein style ("Ravel's *Bolero* is a sort of high-class hootchy-kootchy° music"). Some critics grumbled° that this was much too casual, but the public plainly thought otherwise. It became very fashionable to attend the Thursday night concerts. Indeed, all the Bernstein concerts were sold out.

peagreen . . . very new first-year students

sort of music for belly dancers

complained

The critics, and professionals in general, have always done much grumbling about Leonard Bernstein. They did not know what to think of the overpublicized showman who jumped from symphony to musical comedy and from Carnegie Hall to Broadway, who would conduct anything and compose anything—even a score for the movie *On the Waterfront*—who joked, played the piano, and lectured enthusiastically about the Beatles, the genius of Johann Sebastian Bach, or ancient Japanese music. They could not take him seriously. With time, however, they came to realize that he was one of the best contemporary° conductors, particularly for the works of twentieth-century composers like Mahler, Copland, Sibelius, and Stravinsky. And they also recognized that Bernstein could make the most familiar Beethoven symphony sparkle with fresh life.

here, of our own time

Leonard Bernstein

As a composer, Bernstein is not unanimously admired. Few of his critics would deny the popular appeal of his light works—*On the Town* and *West Side Story*, for example. But his symphonic music is judged shallow and imitative. What can you expect, say the most severe of them, from a man who, in his fifties, is still running in all directions at once and wasting his talent aimlessly? Bernstein himself agrees that he needs to narrow his activities. He left the Philharmonic, he said, to concentrate on writing, composing, and perhaps participating in some nonmusical ventures, For some time, perhaps under the influence of John and Robert Kennedy, he was interested in the civil rights struggle and wanted to involve himself directly in it. But in 1970 when he organized a reception in his Park Avenue apartment, with the participation of Black Panther leaders, in order to raise bail money[6] for twelve jailed Panthers, his efforts brought him more criticism and ridicule than satisfaction.

According to Bernstein, traditional symphonic music is dead and contemporary music too mediocre to deserve being championed. As a result the directors of the great symphony orchestras find themselves relegated° to the role of museum put in a low position curators,° with little to do besides preserving the masterpieces person in charge of the past. Although Bernstein does not consider this role unimportant, he would prefer to play a part in the development of theater music, the only musical genre° that, in his opinion, sort, style has a chance to flourish in the future. This is a field in which he has been very successful himself, with his *West Side Story* in 1957. He thinks that there will be an evolution of the American theater form, "increasingly serious, but always in the vernacular."° It is not by chance that he has been conducting ordinary language many operas in the United States, in Italy, and in Austria, or that he has been recording *Carmen*.

Neither is it by chance that his first important work after he left the Philharmonic, *Mass* (1970), was a drama, a sort of supershow involving symphonic musicians, folk musicians, actors, singers, narrators, and dancers. *Mass* surprised audiences and critics. One chic° listener found it "less interesting fashionable, elegant than *Hair*," and another one described it as "chaotic,° cheap, a completely confused kind of religious *West Side Story*." But the music critic of the *New Yorker*, Winthrop Sargeant, was charmed. He found it "a

[6]Money paid to a court to free an accused person, which is returned when the person appears for trial.

rare thing, a stunning° and absorbing modern composition that   *impressively beautiful*
can reach the heart of any musical audience. In spite of my
pessimism about the state of contemporary music, this work
has given me hope. I was surprised by the real originality of the
score."

Bernstein's loyal audience has not lost him entirely. He will
still appear with the Philharmonic for several concerts and for a
new series of Young People's Concerts on television. It would
be a great loss if he were to stop lecturing and writing.
Controversial as he may be as a composer, as a conductor and
teacher he has few peers. And he loves to teach. He teaches "all
the time," complains his daughter Jamie. "Just ask him what
'Existentialism'° means, and you get a lecture for the rest of the   *pessimistic philosophical doctrine*
day, starting with the meaning of the word in Greek!" His
favorite subject is music, naturally. With his relaxed humor, his   *doing and saying amusing and foolish things*
singing, his clowning,° his genius for making clear and
enjoyable anything from rock-and-roll to Gregorian chant,[7]
Bernstein has been able to fascinate crowds of nonmusical
people, including many a protesting little boy dragged to the
concert hall by a dutiful mother. Equally delightful and
informative are his books, *The Joy of Music* and *The Infinite
Variety of Music.* There is no doubt that he is a born educator.
In fact, one is tempted to agree retrospectively° with Samuel   *looking back in time*
Bernstein: if Aunt Clara had not left that piano behind, Lenny
would have made a first-class rabbi.

---

[7]Vocal religious music dating from the time of Pope Gregory I (540–604 A.D.).

Questions

1. How did young Leonard Bernstein discover music?
2. Why did his father object to having his son become a musician?
3. What qualities seem likely to make a winner?
4. What could you say about Bernstein's "facility"?
5. Can he get interested in anything but music?
6. Why does it seem surprising that Bernstein should have studied conducting with Fritz Reiner?
7. How did he happen to conduct the Philharmonic when he was an assistant conductor?
8. What is *Jeremiah*?
9. Who is Jerome Robbins?
10. How did Rodzinski react to his assistant's success?

Vocabulary

A *Repeat the following sentences, replacing the word or phrase in italics with one with similar meaning taken from the list.*

deplore	adapt
discard	restrained
baton	perseverance
facility	immersed
disgruntled	renounce
fiddle	upright
shatter	sway
grimace	get on . . . nerves

1. Clara, having too much furniture, *threw away* some pieces.
2. Lenny soon *irritated* his father with his piano playing.
3. One day Samuel *broke* the piano *in pieces.*
4. Lenny, of course, was *in a very bad humor.*
5. He said that he would *give up* the piano.
6. He played the *violin* instead.
7. He learned with shameful *ease.*
8. He also had plenty of talent, energy, and *persistence.*

B *What is:*

1. harmony?
2. a choreographer?
3. an opera?
4. a duet?
5. a rabbi?
6. a podium?
7. a baton?
8. a score?

Structures

A **Examples** I would not want to run against him.
This is a man against whom I would not want to run.

I borrowed many scores from him.
This is a man from whom I borrowed many scores.

1. Lenny went to school with him.
2. He owes much to him.
3. He received excellent advice from him.
4. He has a great deal of affection for him.
5. He would not have succeeded without him.
6. He will never say anything against him.
7. He once substituted for him.
8. He dedicated a concerto to him.

B **Example** Lenny went off to Harvard.
Off to Harvard went Lenny!

1. The conductor marched up to the podium.
2. His baton went up.
3. The orchestra went "Blam."
4. The conductor jumped up and down.
5. The baton flew into the lap of a woman.
6. The woman marched out of the concert hall.

Topics for Discussion or Written Assignment

1. What is a charismatic person? Whom do you consider charismatic among today's public figures? How does one go about acquiring charisma?
2. Name a piece of music or a tune that you like particularly, and explain why you like it.

3. Every child should be taught music as they are taught the three R's. Yes or no? Why?
4. Have you ever heard the music accompanying a television show or a movie while you could not see the screen, and guessed pretty well what was going on (danger, romance, motion, sunset, discovery of the crime, or anything else)? How does music describe? Give examples if you can.
5. Does music affect people's mood? How?

Exercises for Section II pp. 72-77

Questions

1. Why did Koussevitzsky think that he should admonish Bernstein?
2. How did Bernstein meet Maria Callas?
3. What seems to be necessary to make a great orchestra?
4. When Bernstein gave his first Thursday night concert, some of the members of the audience and some critics may have been shocked. Why?
5. How did the members of the Philharmonic judge Bernstein professionally?
6. Which of Bernstein's compositions can you name?
7. How good does he seem to be as a composer?
8. What does Bernstein think of contemporary music?
9. What kind of music does he see flourishing in the future?
10. Why do some professionals criticize him? Can you think of another reason?

Vocabulary

A 1. The man in charge of a museum is a _____.
2. The person who reads or tells the story in a show or a film is the _____.
3. When a show uses everyday language, it is written in the _____.
4. A fairy uses her _____ to turn a pumpkin into a carriage.
5. A _____ decision is a decision taken by several people who are all of the same opinion.
6. A composer who lives in the same period of time as we do is a _____ composer.

B 1. Bernstein wanted to turn his first ballet into a longer show; he _____ it into a musical.

2. Koussevitzsky thought that Leonard was making a mistake; he _____ him.

3. Bernstein always brings success to his orchestras; he makes them _____.

4. When you are afraid, you _____.

5. Bernstein does not want to be _____ to the role of museum curator.

6. He thinks that modern music is too mediocre to deserve being _____.

C *Fill the blanks with the noun suggested by the verb or adjective in italics.*

Example Samuel Bernstein was surprised that his son should have been *so successful.* But of course he was delighted by his **success.**

1. Only an *excellent* conductor could impress the musicians of the Philharmonic. They soon recognized Bernstein's _____.

2. They had known him since he *replaced* Bruno Walter for a concert. At the time of the _____, they already liked his conducting.

3. He seldom had time *to compose* at leisure. Some of his _____ do sound rather too hasty.

4. Bernstein *discovered* opera when he was thirteen. He was completely fascinated by his _____.

5. He is a very *loyal* friend. In turn he can count on his old friends' _____.

6. He *conducts* very exuberantly. It is difficult to believe that he learned _____ from the restrained Fritz Reiner.

Structures

A **Example** Bernstein has much to do; he finds life very exciting.
The more Bernstein has to do, **the more exciting** he finds life.

1. Bernstein heard much about Maria Callas; he became interested in meeting her.

2. He received much publicity; the critics felt suspicious of him.

3. Bernstein hears much contemporary music; he finds it appalling.

4. The orchestra made many tours abroad; the musicians were pleased with their conductor.

5. I hear many opinions about Bernstein's *Mass;* I am getting very confused about it.

6. He has heard it many times; he finds it very chaotic.

B   **Example**   He is controversial as a composer, but he has few peers as a conductor.

Controversial as he may be as a composer, he has few peers as a conductor.

1. He is cocky, but he is more than a showman.
2. Callas is difficult, but she accepted a justified cut in her arias.
3. *Mass* is interesting, but it is difficult to like the first time.
4. Bernstein is sure of himself, but he did not know how the musicians would accept him.
5. The musicians are individually excellent, but they do not make an excellent orchestra because they are not disciplined.
6. He is extremely successful, but he is not original.

Topics for Discussion or Written Assignment

1. Do you know what *West Side Story* is about? Have you seen it? Do you know the music? What do you think of it?
2. What opinion have you formed of Leonard Bernstein as a person and as a musician? Do you like him? Why?
3. Are the Beatles good musicians? Did they deserve their fame? Why?
4. After reading only the titles of Leonard Bernstein's compositions, can you make some guesses about their character, their content, or the composer's personality?

J. Robert Oppenheimer

Born April 22, 1904
In New York, New York
Died February 18, 1966

I n 1953 Robert Oppenheimer reached his forty-ninth
birthday. He was no longer the young genius who had awed his
elders with the depth and swiftness of his mind and with the
extent of his culture. He had become the most celebrated
nuclear physicist in the world, a legendary figure, perhaps too
often put on a pedestal.° For several years after the end of the   column on which a
statue stands
Second World War, he wielded an enormous influence as chief
scientific advisor to his government. Too much influence, some
whispered. His power had decreased in the fifties, and in 1952
he had resigned from his position as chairman of the General
Advisory Committee of the Atomic Energy Commission. But he
remained a consultant° to the AEC, and, more impor-   one who advises on
special matters
tant, he was director of the Institute for Advanced Study at
Princeton. To the general public he was mostly known as "the
father of the atom bomb," a title he disliked because he found it
grossly oversimplified. Besides, he was not very happy with his
child.

Oppenheimer traveled extensively° in the summer and fall of   widely, broadly
1953. He delivered a series of lectures in Brazil, made a speech   honorary . . . academic
in England, and received one more honorary degree,° this time   title given for special
distinction
from Oxford University. After the ceremonies, he and his wife,
Kitty, flew to Paris for a reunion with their old friend Haakon
Chevalier, then to Denmark to see another old friend, physicist
Niels Bohr. The Oppenheimers returned to the United States in
mid-December, just in time for a happy Christmas with their
young son and daughter. And there the sky crashed on their
heads.

Early in November, J. Edgar Hoover, director of the Federal
Bureau of Investigation (FBI), had received a letter from a
William L. Borden, a former member of a congressional staff
who had access to° security files. The study of Oppenheimer's   had . . . was allowed to
see
file, Borden wrote, had led him to conclude that the famous
physicist was an agent of the Soviets. Although no proof or
evidence was offered, Hoover sent the letter and the file to
President Eisenhower, who immediately ordered that "a blank
wall" be placed at once between Oppenheimer and all
classified° information until the AEC could investigate his   kept secret
loyalty.

84

The Oppenheimers had just returned home when Robert learned that the new chairman of the AEC, Admiral Lewis L. Strauss, wanted to see him. He knew Strauss very well. They had both been connected with the AEC since its creation in 1946. But they were not friends. They had clashed° many times on matters of national security and on the question of the hydrogen bomb, which Oppenheimer had never warmly endorsed.° Always extremely concerned about the danger of Russian aggression, Strauss had been an early supporter of the superweapon. For him and for men like Borden, there was something suspicious in Oppenheimer's reluctant° attitude toward the bomb. Why, the man had even said that the United States should renounce it forever, on the eccentric° notion that the Soviet Union would follow the good example!

At some other period of history, such ideas would have been regarded as the dreams of a naive° egghead.° But 1953 was a bad year for naiveté. Senator Joseph McCarthy's anticommunist crusade was in full swing, choking the country with suspicion and fear. McCarthy had won his reelection in 1950 on the promise that he would rid the United States of all the communist traitors who, according to him, had infiltrated° the State Department, the Defense Department, and indeed all government agencies. Waving lists of names—never quite close enough to be read—he had been accusing and destroying "Reds," real and imaginary, without bothering much about facts and proof. It was all too easy, unfortunately, to believe him. The once-trusted Russian ally was now recognized for what it was: a ruthless, deceitful adversary. A large spy ring operating for Russia had been uncovered in Canada, and in 1950 it had been revealed that Klaus Fuchs, one of the British scientists who had worked on the American atom bomb and on the hydrogen bomb, had passed his knowledge to the Russians. Scientists did not look reliable in those days; the Borden letter had been mailed at the right time to be taken seriously.

Four days before Christmas, Lewis Strauss and Oppenheimer met in the AEC building in Washington. After a feeble° attempt at small talk, the admiral came to the point of the meeting: Oppenheimer's security clearance° had been suspended, and there was a letter listing the charges against him. Oppenheimer, the admiral added, had twenty-four hours to decide whether he wanted to resign from his position as consultant or to face a security board to clear his name and

conflicted, fought

supported

unwilling, unenthusiastic

very different

simple, childlike/ intellectual

entered quietly

weak

security . . . permission to deal with classified material

possibly have his clearance restored. Dazed,° the physicist left   confused
the building and somehow found his way to the office of a
friend, attorney Joseph Volpe. In his confusion he mislaid° his   lost
beloved pipe, on the way. "I lost my pipe that day," he said
later. "Put it down somewhere and couldn't remember where.
Maybe that sums up about as well as anything my state of
mind."

Since his resignation would have looked like an admission of
guilt, Oppenheimer had no choice but to request a security
hearing, as he pointed out in his reply to the AEC letter. He sent
along a detailed account of his life, which, he thought, would
exonerate° him by putting his actions in their proper context.   prove innocent
By nature and by education, Oppenheimer believed in common
sense and good will. In his view, no misunderstanding could
resist a candid,° logical explanation. At the Ethical Culture   honest, open
School of New York, where he had received his education, he
had been taught that human nature is basically good; that
ignorant or misinformed as people may be at times, they will
always bow° to reason if they are given the proper explana-   yield, submit
tions. Young Robert had never doubted the truth of this
dogma.° Why should he have? Nothing had ever happened in   belief taught as truth by an authority
his family cocoon° to shake his belief. His wealthy, German-   protective covering
born father and his artistic mother were gentle, open-minded°   receptive, free from prejudice
intellectuals, attentive to the happiness of their two sons,
particularly the brilliant Robert.

It had been apparent early that Robert had received more
than his share of intelligence. He was alarmingly precocious.°   unusually advanced
At six, he had become seriously interested in rocks; at eleven
he was elected as the only nonadult member to the New York
Mineralogical° Society, and at twelve he had delivered his first   having to do with the study of rocks
paper there. A frail° child, solemn and a bit prissy,° he learned   not strong / too proper, too refined
with astounding speed and retained everything. He was not
one to hide his superiority. "Ask me a question in Latin," he
would say cockily to his older cousins. "I'll answer it in
Greek." The most annoying part of the boast was that he was
perfectly able to do as he said.

Courses and classmates never presented any challenge to
him, and he had plenty of time and energy to spare on
extracurricular° learning of his own. After taking all the   outside the school program
available courses in mathematics and sciences, plus advanced
courses in Latin, Greek, French, and German, he graduated

from high school in 1921 in a firework of straight A's. It took him only three years at Harvard to end up with a master's degree in science *summa cum laude.*° What to do next? He had played at various times with the notion of becoming a writer, or perhaps a painter or a chemist or an architect. But while at Harvard he found himself attracted by the "new" physics, which was nuclear physics. With the discovery of radioactivity and of the structure of the atom, physics had become, since the turn of the century, a fresh, adventurous field. It was challenging; it was exciting; it was wide open. It was also appealing to Robert's artistic temperament, because he saw in it "the study of order, of regularity, of what makes matter harmonious and what makes it work."

Latin, with highest praise

There were not many centers for advanced study in atomic physics at the time, and none in America. Robert crossed the Atlantic to work in two of the best: the Cavendish laboratory at Cambridge, England, and the old University of Göttingen in Germany. The small and ancient town of Göttingen was then attracting all the students interested in the "new" mathematics and in the "new" physics. From all over the world bright young men flocked° to the lectures of professors James Franck and Max Born. There Robert met many of the young scientists who were to be his friends, his associates, or his opponents throughout his life: the Belgian Paul Dirac, the Italian Enrico Fermi, the German Hans Bethe, the Hungarians Leo Szilard, John von Neumann, and Edward Teller, and many others.

gathered in great numbers

Even in such company Robert Oppenheimer stood out as an extraordinary being. Not only was he a dazzling° thinker in his own discipline,° but he was perfectly at ease in a number of other fields. He was an authority on world history and literature, a master of the English language, a student of Eastern religions, psychology, and all sciences, and a connoisseur° of paintings and wines. He dominated all conversations and all courses, often to an annoying extent. He was fluent in five languages, and as if that were not enough, he mastered Italian in one month, while working on his arduous° doctorate, just because he wanted to read and discuss Dante's *Divine Comedy* in the original language. Besides, he was a poet. That was too much for Paul Dirac. "I hear," he exploded one day, "that you write poetry as well as working at physics. How on earth can you do two such things at once? In sciences one tries to tell

brilliant enough to blind

field of work

expert

very difficult

people something that no one knew before in such a way as to be understood by everyone. But in poetry it's the exact opposite!"

The fact was that there were several Robert Oppenheimers. There was the clear-minded physicist, and there was the mystic steeped° in Hindu philosophy, who at thirty would learn Sanskrit to better enjoy the sacred epic of the Hindus, the *Bhagavad-Gita*. There was the gourmet° fond of fine dishes and expensive wines, and there was the ascetic° who spent his summers in the burnt hills of New Mexico, happy to sleep on the ground after riding his horse all day and eating, when he remembered to eat at all, harsh foods that ruined his digestion for life. There was the quiet scholar, and there was the daredevil° who mounted difficult horses and loved to sail his boat in the worst Atlantic storms. There was the shy thoughtful gentleman, and there was the gay bachelor who was the life of parties. There was the diplomat who ruled smoothly over a battalion of touchy geniuses during the war, and there was the arrogant "intellectual snob"° who went out of his way to hurt and humiliate even his friends. That particular Robert was to make many bitter enemies, including a Secretary of the Air Force, his fellow scientist Edward Teller, and Admiral Lewis Strauss.

Oppenheimer received his doctorate in June 1927 with distinction. "Phew!" sighed Professor James Franck after giving him his final oral examination. "I am glad that's over. He was on the point of questioning *me*." For two more years the young doctor worked at Caltech (the California Institute of Technology), in Switzerland, and at the University of Leyden, Holland, where he made a sensation by delivering his lectures in Dutch. It was at Leyden that he received his durable nickname "Opje," pronounced Oppie. In 1928, overcome by homesickness, he went back to the United States and spent another happy summer in New Mexico, where he bought a primitive ranch. He was ready to start a teaching career.

II

Oppenheimer had already acquired such an extraordinary reputation in scientific circles that he could take his choice: a dozen great universities were offering him their students and

steeped° filled with

gourmet° expert on food
ascetic° one who lives without pleasures or comforts

daredevil° very bold, reckless person

intellectual snob° person who feels superior to others

their laboratories. He finally selected the University of California at Berkeley because, he explained, he was delighted by the collection of sixteenth- and seventeenth-century French poetry in the library. There was also, at the head of the Department of Physics, a man as young and as enthusiastic about nuclear physics as he was himself, Ernest O. Lawrence. Oppenheimer promptly made friends with him and with many members of the faculty, including an instructor in the Department of Romance Languages named Haakon Chevalier, who was known as a leftist in politics and even suspected of being a communist.

In the course of the next few years Oppenheimer built Berkeley into a major center of scientific study, equal to the old European institutes. It is very simple: in those years the path to the highest work in theoretical physics[1] passed through Oppie's arduous seminars.° Demanding, impatient, sarcastic,° he was not an easy teacher. Moreover, it had never occurred to him that not everyone could think at his speed, and he did not notice that his students had difficulty following his swift and lofty° explanations. They were not alone in that respect; the faculty was wrestling with the same problem. One day, after a working session among physicists that Oppenheimer had missed, Lawrence beamed:° "I am glad that Robert was not there. He would have settled everything in thirty seconds and we would have had to go on before anyone else really understood the issue."

Oppenheimer's students worshiped him. Nothing like it had ever been seen on campus, and to outsiders it looked ridiculous. Oppie's young men followed him everywhere and took notes in relay° to be sure to preserve his smallest utterances.° They copied him: his odd walk; his hunched shoulders; his speech habits; his way of saying, "It's like so. . . ." Like him they chain-smoked° or chewed on a pipe; like him they jumped, lighter in hand, the moment someone took a cigarette out of a pack. They worked with him at all hours, day and night, and shared his pleasures. He took them to restaurants, introduced them to wines, chamber music, and esoteric° poetry; he advised them on romantic entanglements.° Come spring, they would all follow him to Caltech, where he lectured for a semester. Most of them reenrolled the next year to

study groups / mocking, sneering

on a very high level

smiled broadly

in turns

sayings

lit one cigarette from the preceding one

difficult to understand / complications

[1]The branch of physics dealing with general theories, as opposed to experimental physics, which deals with actual experiments and research.

take his course all over again. This magnetism° of Oppenheim-   *strong attraction*
er's worked not only on students but on much older men as
well, and one of the arguments brought against him during his
security hearing was that his power over people made him
extremely dangerous.

At Berkeley Oppenheimer found out that some kind of life
was actually going on outside of laboratories and lecture halls.
He had never been curious about it before. He never read
newspapers, never listened to the radio. Current events were of
so little interest to him that he lived through the winter of 1929
without knowing about the stock market collapse.° Gradually,   *complete breakdown*
however, he came to notice the grim° financial problems with   *hard and sad*
which some of his students had to struggle. He became aware
that they could not find jobs, even with their Ph.D.'s. From his
German relatives he was also learning about the hardships that
they—and all the other Jews in Germany—had to endure at the
hands of the Nazis. He knew that the great scientists he   *worshiped, respected deeply*
revered° had been forced out of their laboratories. In 1933
Albert Einstein took refuge in the United States and settled at
the Institute for Advanced Study. Born and Franck, among
others, followed his example. Soon they were joined by
younger men, such as Teller, Bethe, von Neumann, and
Szilard, and by Enrico Fermi when the latter became disgusted
with Mussolini's fascism. And so Oppenheimer began "to
understand how deeply political and economic events could
affect men's lives and to feel the need to participate more fully
in the life of the community."

It was natural that he should turn for direction to the three
people closest to him: his brother Frank, his sister-in-law, and
the young woman with whom he was then in love, Jean
Tatlock. All three happened to be members of the Communist
Party. They introduced him to leftist literature and took him to   *small, narrow/ useless*
meetings that struck him as petty° and futile.° But social
problems touched him. He became active in the Teachers'   *moving from place to place*
Union and in a group concerned with the plight of migrant°
workers. He subscribed to the communist paper, allowed his
name to be used by radical organizations, and contributed to
the Relief Fund for Spanish Loyalists during the Spanish Civil
War. In his letter to the AEC in 1953 he was to make the point
that "many good Americans had been emotionally committed
to the Loyalist cause." Some had gone to Spain to help in the
fight. Among those who died there was a young American

communist married to Kitty Puening, the future Mrs. Robert Oppenheimer. Kitty herself had joined the party to please her first husband, but she disliked the experience and dropped out long before meeting Oppenheimer. For his part, Robert had lost his illusions° and his interest in communism by the time of their marriage in 1940, although he did not stop his financial contributions until 1942.

In that year he was made director of the Manhattan District, the code name given to the development of the atomic bomb. Both as scientist and as administrator, he had a tremendous task to face. To be sure, the uranium nucleus[2] had been split many times in laboratories. But nobody knew how to build a weapon around the phenomenon,° and, once the weapon was built, how to prevent it from disintegrating° the whole planet. The gathering and coordination of all the experts necessary for the project was quite a feat in itself. In the opinion of men who helped develop the bomb, the choice of Robert Oppenheimer as director was the best that could have been made. Nobody had his degree of intelligence nor his ability to grasp problems, to disentangle scientific knots, and to think "at the speed of light." "The man always gave you the answer before you had time to express the question," said one brilliant member of the team, the physicist Lauritsen.

Another sensational asset° of Oppenheimer's was his "intellectual sex appeal," which made the top men eager to work with him. This attraction became obvious as soon as he started gathering the men who would work for the Manhattan District. The best physicists and mathematicians happily followed him to the hot, remote mesa° he had selected at Los Alamos, New Mexico, to work far from curious eyes. Hans Bethe went; so did Richard Feynman, Edward Teller, von Neumann, James Franck, and dozens of other great minds. With Oppie in charge, the building of the atom bomb seemed the most intriguing° and fascinating intellectual venture in the world. Work went on round the clock,° in such spirited and casual fashion that extrovert Edward Teller would feel perfectly free to explain a difficult experiment to his colleagues in the form of an off-color° limerick.°

Oppie, the soul of it all, was everywhere, working with everybody, listening to personal complaints and scientific

mistaken ideas

remarkable fact

breaking into pieces, destroying

valuable possession

high ground, high plateau

interesting, curious

round . . . twenty-four hours a day

improper / humorous short poem

[2]Central part of an atom of uranium, consisting of neutrons (particles without electric charge) and protons (particles with a positive charge).

equations, probing,° explaining, clarifying, suggesting new °searching deeply
lines of research, and handling everything from technical
problems to discontented wives. "He was magnificent,"
commented all members of the team later; and they all stressed
his enormous scientific contribution and the tact that he
displayed then. "But there was something else," said one. "The
mesa as he created it enlarged the most unexpected variety of
careers in science. A certain magic, romance, devotion, cause
people who were there to remember it as the most significant
part of their lives."

One group of men who did not find Oppenheimer
magnificent at all was the counterintelligence force° responsi- °group guarding secrets against spies
ble for the security of the Manhattan District. From their point
of view, the multilingual° collection of genial crackpots° °speaking many languages / crazy people
working at Los Alamos was already quite distressing. One of
them—Fermi—even belonged to a country that was at war with
the United States! But the information collected about their
director was enough to give nightmares to the whole FBI. After
a horrified survey of Oppie's recent political adventures, the
security men demanded his immediate dismissal and found
themselves colliding° head on with the Army boss of the °running into
project, General Leslie B. Groves. The stout general felt as
strongly as anyone about security, but, having come to know
Oppie very well, he felt that the man could be trusted.
Eccentric or not, this particular crackpot was a loyal citizen
and, rarer yet, a man who knew how to keep secrets. Besides,
he was indispensable.° He would stay. Security had to retreat °absolutely necessary
and be content with keeping an eye on Oppenheimer, opening
his mail, bugging° his telephone, and following him wherever °tapping
he went. Nothing significant turned up, except one small
episode that would become known as "the Chevalier incident."

Oppenheimer had not found it necessary to drop those of his °favoring rapid and deep changes / tendencies, sympathies
friends who had radical° leanings° when he dropped commu-
nism. He still liked Haakon Chevalier, who was amusing and
kind. Just before moving to Los Alamos, the Oppenheimers
invited the Chevaliers for dinner, and, in the course of the
evening, while the two men were alone together, Chevalier
reported a conversation he had had with a communist engineer
named George Eltenton. Eltenton, he said, was wondering if
Oppenheimer would be likely to pass technical information to
his colleagues and allies, the Russian scientists. Oppie was

shocked. "But it would be treason," he said. Chevalier uncomfortably agreed, and they changed the subject.

Sure that his friend had not realized what he was doing, Oppenheimer did not report the incident to his security officer, as he should have. Only eight months later, while discussing another problem, did he mention that George Eltenton should be watched because he had tried to get information "from several physicists at Los Alamos." To Oppenheimer's surprise, the advice was not accepted without further inquiries. After numerous interrogations (that were taped without his knowledge), he was finally and painfully forced to admit that only one physicist—himself—had been approached and that his friend Chevalier had served as intermediary. General Groves and the top security officer, Colonel Landsdale, decided that Oppenheimer's deception had been negligent° rather than   careless criminal, and the matter rested there. But his lie and the delay in reporting the conversation with Chevalier remained noted in Oppenheimer's security file. They were to play a very important part in his fate.

III

The Los Alamos team exploded the first atom bomb on July 16, 1945, near Alamogordo, New Mexico. On August 7 and 9, numbers two and three were dropped over Hiroshima and Nagasaki, and on August 10 Japan surrendered. The war was over. Few of the Manhattan scientists rejoiced over the success of their labor. They had been horrified by the power of the bomb, which had turned out to be much more destructive than had been anticipated. A number of them rushed to Washington to plead° for a tight civilian control of atomic energy. Although   ask earnestly, beg he shared their distress, Oppenheimer did not join in their campaign; he had a more ambitious dream to promote.° The   push (fig.) wisest solution, he felt, was to share atomic secrets with all nations, renounce the bomb, and concentrate on the beneficial°   helpful uses of nuclear energy. As a first step, there should be a formal agreement between the two giant nations, the United States and the Soviet Union, to give up nuclear weapons and allow some kind of inspection of their research installations.

Before long, Oppie was in a position to present his dream to the right people. He had resigned from the Manhattan District in October 1945, and resumed° his teaching at Caltech. But the Truman administration, faced with the awesome° problems of the atomic era, naturally turned for advice to the foremost expert in the field. Soon Oppenheimer was in Washington teaching physics to high officials, talking to the President, calling the department secretaries by their first names, and chairing° the most important committees. It did not take him long to realize that his notion of international cooperation was hopeless; there was not enough trust among big nations, and the question of inspection, for one, raised impossible difficulties.

started again

inspiring awe and fear

being chairman of

Under Oppie's direction, a State Department committee came up with an alternative. Oppenheimer's idea was to make nuclear energy "safe" by putting it entirely in the hands of an international authority that would own the mines of fissionable° substances, control all research, and publish the results for all to see. Thus the fission of the nucleus could never again be used to kill. Instead, it would help humanity, as Oppenheimer and his fellow scientists had hoped from the start.

usable for nuclear reaction

The proposal, presented to the United Nations Atomic Energy Commission, collapsed against Russian opposition. There was no choice but to deal with the atom nationally and to keep ahead of possible enemies. To that end the Atomic Energy Commission was created in 1946. Lewis Strauss was one of the nine commissioners, and Robert Oppenheimer was chairman of the General Advisory Board, which would have to inform and counsel the commission on scientific matters.

The nomination brought up the question of Oppenheimer's loyalty and the Chevalier incident all over again. Not everybody felt comfortable with Oppie's past. Once again his indiscretions° were investigated, and once again they were dismissed as insignificant in view of his accomplishments, his absolute discretion at Los Alamos, and his present political attitude, now completely anti-Soviet. J. Edgar Hoover himself closed the FBI file, and Lewis Strauss was one of those who voted in favor of Oppie's selection. In 1947 the admiral gave another proof of his esteem° for the controversial physicist: he offered him the position of director of the Institute for Advanced Study, of which he was a trustee. Oppie accepted and moved to Princeton.

unwise actions

high regard

Second atom bomb test, Bikini Lagoon in the Pacific Ocean, July 24, 1946.

For the next few years, Oppenheimer, consulted by policymakers, revered by all as the number one intellectual in the land, stood at the top of his fame and of his power. He enjoyed it thoroughly. There was little time left for physics, but he was happy to lecture his fellow Americans on radio and television about the wonders and the dangers of modern science and about the desirability of an honest, open world where men would communicate freely and reason together.

He was still suspect to many people, and his speeches did not help. The uneasy atmosphere of the McCarthy era had spread all over the country. Besides, the Russians now had an atom bomb. The future was looking bleak° and international communism threatening. Oppenheimer, accused more or less directly, was again questioned several times. He was always watched. Once he remarked laughingly that the FBI was spending more money bugging his telephone than he had received for his work at Los Alamos. In 1949, when the AEC was accused of selling fissionable material to Norway, Oppenheimer was called to testify before a Senate committee

° cold, unattractive

on the matter. He explained that the radium isotopes[3] sold to Norway could not possibly help that nation build atomic weapons. But in the course of his explanations he could not resist the temptation of making a fool of Lewis Strauss, who had objected noisily to the sale of the isotopes. The admiral was never to forget or forgive his humiliation.

Strauss was not the only man irritated by Oppenheimer at that time. There were others who had suffered from his sharp tongue and his callous° lack of consideration° for other people's egos. There were those who resented his negative attitude toward the hydrogen bomb. Such was the case with Edward Teller, Edward Lawrence, and with the other physicists of Berkeley. As early as 1943, Teller had tried to have research done on the hydrogen bomb rather than on the less powerful atom bomb. After Hiroshima, he had renewed his campaign with more vigor. But he had never gained Oppie's support, and he resented it. Like Lawrence, he too increasingly resented Oppie's celebrity and influence.

Oppenheimer had many different objections to the hydrogen bomb. He considered it a dreadful° weapon, overdestructive, sinful. Unlike the nuclear energy of the atom bomb, which had many possible utilizations in biology, medicine, and industry, the thermonuclear energy used in the hydrogen bomb could lead only to one thing: an instrument of death, thousands of times more destructive than the Hiroshima weapon. Also, until 1951 Oppenheimer would not have promoted it simply because he knew that it was not practical; any thermonuclear device built with the knowledge available at that time would have been much too heavy to transport. When a new idea, in 1951, made it possible to build a bomb small enough to be carried by a plane, Oppenheimer became more interested and proclaimed the new solution "fascinating; beautiful and technically sweet." Even so, he declined° to participate in its fabrication.° Worse still, he kept pointing out in his public speeches as well as in his reports that the hydrogen bomb was not only a monstrous° killer, but an unnecessary one. There was hardly any target in Russia large enough for it, and it would be wiser for the United States to build a number of small or medium sized atom bombs that could be used tactically° by the Army, the Navy, and the Air Force.

unfeeling / thought, care

frightening

refused politely

making

causing fear and horror

wherever necessary in battle

[3]Elements with the properties of radium but having slightly different atomic weights.

Such declarations did not please the high command of the Air Force, who had no desire to share the atomic weapons with the other services, and who disliked Oppie's other proposals for a defense system in Canada and for atomic submarines. Also indignant were men like Lewis Strauss and William Borden, who believed that the best weapon could only be the biggest one. When he learned that the Russians had exploded their hydrogen bomb ahead of the Americans in August 1953, Borden "understood" the reasons behind Oppenheimer's diverse° objections to the bomb—he had been using delaying   various
tactics to allow his Russian friends to gain an advantage over the United States. Borden then wrote his letter to J. Edgar Hoover. When the president consulted Lewis Strauss, who was his scientific advisor, on the Oppenheimer problem, the admiral made no effort to reassure him about Oppie's loyalty.

The security hearing "in the matter of J. Robert Oppenheimer" opened on April 12, 1954, and for three terrible weeks the three members of the board searched Oppenheimer's private and public life. Essentially, they had to determine whether he was a security risk, because of his character, his associations, or his lack of loyalty. His involvement with radical groups in the late 1930s had been included in the AEC's list of charges. He was also accused of hiring former communists for the Manhattan Project, of remaining a friend of radical Haakon Chevalier, and of other such reckless actions that showed his   lack of concern /
arrogant disregard° for security. All this was old hat° for Oppie.   an old story
He had answered those charges time and again, and he had always been cleared, even by Lewis Strauss and by the FBI. The AEC letter offered only one new item, but one that surprised him. He was charged with opposing and hindering° the   making difficult
development of the hydrogen bomb and with failing to make other physicists enthusiastic about it. All of this, it was pointed out, was casting° grave doubts about his loyalty to his country.   throwing

Forty-four witnesses came to testify at the hearings—most of them for the defense. General Groves and Colonel Landsdale had come voluntarily to plead for their former "problem child" of Los Alamos and to explain the Chevalier "lie" as a forgivable indiscretion. Famous men like Hans Bethe and George F. Kennan, former American ambassador to Russia, testified to Oppie's patriotism, his loyalty to the country, his unique value for the United States, and the basic honesty of his character.

There was only one important scientific figure among the

witnesses for the prosecution. It was Edward Teller, who was then working on the hydrogen bomb. Asked if he considered Oppenheimer a security risk, Teller replied that "he would like to see the interests of the country in hands which [he] understood better." "I would feel personally more secure," he added, "if public matters would rest in other hands." For this damning° answer—which was to weigh heavily on the final verdict°—Teller paid by years of hostility from his fellow scientists, who held him responsible for Oppenheimer's downfall.

very damaging

decision of a tribunal

By a vote of two to one, the members of the board reluctantly recommended that the security clearance be denied to the "father of the atom bomb" because of his disregard for security rules, his dangerous associations, and his attitude in the matter of the hydrogen bomb. His loyalty, the report explained at great length, was not at all in question. He had proved it by years of service to the United States, and he had always exhibited° an unusual ability to keep vital secrets to himself. The final verdict of the AEC, written by Lewis Strauss and published in June, had a harsher sound. Oppenheimer was denied clearance, it said, because of "fundamental defects"° in his character, as demonstrated by the "fabrication of lies" in the Chevalier incident.

shown

flaws, faults

The report upset the press and the scientific world. Famous columnists called the hearings a farce,° a kangaroo court,° a shameful inquisition.° They protested against the unfairness of the procedure and the shabby° tactics of the prosecuting attorney.° They pointed out that it was illegal to punish a man for charges of which he had already been cleared. To this day the Oppenheimer case remains controversial, although the balance now inclines in his favor. Books, articles, and dramas are still written about the case. The angle varies, the villains° change. Some authors blame the mood of the McCarthy era, others the jealousy of Edward Teller or the vindictiveness° of Lewis Strauss and others. Some hold to the opinion that Oppenheimer was pushed aside because he was running against powerful opponents in the matter of the hydrogen bomb and because he was still too influential and dangerous to them. There are also those who still consider him a traitor—justly punished.

ridiculous joke/ irregular court outside of the law
Catholic court established to find and condemn heretics
mean, unfair
prosecuting . . . lawyer in charge of the accusation

evil men in a story or play

desire for revenge

Whatever° the case, Robert Oppenheimer was never again allowed to serve his government. He retired to Princeton and until his death applied himself to the development of the Institute for Advanced Study. He never recovered from the ordeal of the hearings; he had been too deeply hurt, and, besides, there was, among all the Robert Oppenheimers, a man who had relished° power and who missed it. But the lover of science and the teacher had the opportunity to enjoy a measure of happiness. As always, Oppenheimer's presence at the Institute attracted the greatest scientific talents, and during his directorship the Institute—until then mostly devoted to mathematics and historical study—became a high center of theoretical physics. Too much so, in the view of the mathematicians. Oppie's personal reputation and influence among scientists and intellectuals had gained, rather than suffered, from his official disgrace. He was still receiving honors and invitations to participate in scientific events all over the world. As the years went by and the political climate changed, Oppenheimer was progressively brought back into public view. In 1963 President Kennedy ventured° to invite him to a dinner honoring a group of Nobel Prize winners at the White House. There were some protests, but the president nevertheless awarded him the Enrico Fermi Award "for his contribution to the national atomic strength." More would have been done eventually, perhaps, but three years later Oppenheimer died of cancer of the throat.

 His death was a great loss not only for the United States but for the entire world, because men of such intellectual power truly belong to the whole of humanity. Oppie loved his country deeply; he could not remain out of it too long, and after his disgrace he could not bring himself to accept Prime Minister Nehru's invitation to live and work in India. In spite of his patriotism, however, he thought more in terms of mankind than in terms of nations. He was a philosopher who, as his friend Hans Bethe remarked, "worked at physics because he found physics the best way to do philosophy." He was in a class apart, like Albert Einstein, but unlike Einstein he never made any tremendous discovery. It has often been noted that he had never received, nor deserved, a Nobel Prize. But many of his former students did, and in a way their Nobel Prizes and their contributions were his great accomplishment. Oppenheimer was a supreme guide, a catalyst,[4] a man who had the

°enjoyed greatly

°dared, took the risk

[4]A substance that starts or helps a reaction without taking part in the reaction itself.

vision to define problems more clearly than anyone else and who opened to others the ways to the solutions. Beyond science, he also had a unique ability to open the minds of other men to a total appreciation of the world and to bring to it a spark that even the most intelligent would probably not have had without him.

Questions

1. For what single accomplishment will Robert Oppenheimer most likely be remembered?
2. What kind of trouble started for him in November 1953?
3. Why were men like Borden and Strauss suspicious of Oppenheimer?
4. Why was 1953 "a bad year for naiveté"?
5. Why was it so easy to believe what Senator McCarthy had to say about the danger of communism?
6. Why didn't Oppenheimer resign?
7. What kind of family background did Oppenheimer have?
8. Why could even bright people think that Oppenheimer, as a young man, was just "too much"?
9. Why did nuclear physics look so beautiful to him?
10. How did Dirac compare science and poetry?
11. How did Oppenheimer come to be called Oppie?
12. What made Oppenheimer return to the United States after working in Switzerland and in Holland?

Vocabulary

A
1. Very often, statues are put on a _____.
2. A man whose job it is to advise an organization on certain matters that he knows well is a _____.
3. A man who lives by choice without pleasures or comforts can be called an _____.
4. A belief taught as truth by some authority like a school or a church is a _____.
5. A cocoon is _____.
6. A connoisseur is _____.
7. A gourmet is _____.
8. An egghead is _____.

B
1. If somebody tells you that you are too *touchy*, what does he mean?
2. If he tells you that you are *naive*, what do you understand him to mean?
3. Is it good or bad for an accused man to be *exonerated*? Why?
4. What is a *precocious* child?
5. Is it a good quality to be *open-minded*? Why?

6. Is it easy to hear someone who has a very *feeble* voice?
7. If you are told that a man has traveled *extensively,* does it mean that:
   a) he has just come back from his trip?
   b) he has been in many places?
   c) he has spent a great deal of money on a trip?
   d) he had a good time on his trip?
8. Which is the more *dazzling* light, the sun's or the moon's?
9. What do you think the members of a *mineralogical* society do?
10. Why do you need a clearance to have access to *classified* material?

Structures

A **Example** He said, "Place a blank wall between Oppenheimer and all classified information."
He ordered that a blank wall be placed between Oppenheimer and all classified information.

1. He said, "Examine the security files again."
2. He said, "Call Oppenheimer immediately."
3. He said, "Suspend Oppenheimer's clearance until investigation."
4. He said, "Send that letter to him right away."
5. He said, "Investigate all the scientists who worked on the project."
6. He said, "Hold a security hearing as soon as possible."

B **Example** From the study of the file, he concluded that Oppenheimer was a spy.
The study of the file **led him to conclude** that Oppenheimer was a spy.

1. From his previous experiences, he believed that all men are good and sensible.
2. Because of his fear of the Russians, Strauss supported the development of the hydrogen bomb.
3. From his observations, he had concluded that all scientists are very naive politically.
4. Because of his friends' admiration, Oppie thought that everyone would accept his superiority in the same way.
5. Because of his own open-mindedness, he thought that men only wish to understand and accept.
6. Because of Strauss' small talk, he believed that this would be a friendly meeting.

Topics for Discussion or Written Assignment

1. Snobs. Do you know a snob? In what way is he or she a snob? Is snobbism always directed toward people who are considered inferior? Are we all snobs in some way? Are you a snob? In what ways?
2. Oppenheimer's personality was full of contradictions. Was he unusual in that respect? Was he just like "everybody else"? Is it desirable to have a very complex personality? Dangerous?
3. Do you think that human nature is basically good? Do you think that men usually bow to reason above all things? Should young people be taught that human nature is good and reasonable?
4. What do you think of Oppenheimer's idea of renouncing the bomb and letting Russia (or any other country if there had been any others equipped with atom bombs) follow the good example? Was he very naive, very wise, or a traitor? Should his advice have been taken? What do you think would have happened?

Exercises for Section II   pp. 88-93

Questions

1. Did Oppenheimer say that he had selected Berkeley for scientific reasons?
2. Was there a possible scientific reason?
3. Why was he a difficult teacher?
4. How did the students respond to him?
5. How did Oppenheimer come to notice what was happening in the world?
6. Why did he get involved in leftist activities?
7. What kind of causes did he get interested in?
8. Was his wife a communist?
9. What was the Manhattan District?
10. Why was Oppenheimer such a good choice as director of the District?
11. Why were the security men so nervous about the group working on the project?
12. Who was Haakon Chevalier?
13. How would you sum up the "Chevalier incident"?
14. What did Oppenheimer do that was wrong?
15. Why did General Groves not ask for Oppenheimer's resignation when he heard about the Chevalier incident?

Vocabulary

A 1. A seminar is
  a) a school for priests and ministers
  b) an examination
  c) a study group

  2. A phenomenon is
  a) a remarkable fact
  b) a nuclear reaction
  c) a mistake

  3. A mesa is
  a) what they call a girl in New Mexico
  b) a low plain in New Mexico
  c) a high plateau in New Mexico

  4. A limerick is
  a) an Irishman
  b) a humorous poem
  c) a laboratory scale

  5. A crackpot is
  a) an eccentric
  b) a broken jar
  c) a type of container used in laboratories

B 1. When would you say that a person is *sarcastic*?
  2. What is an *esoteric* poem?
  3. What is a *futile* undertaking?
  4. What is the difference between a *negligent* action and a *criminal* action?
  5. A person, an idea, or an attitude can be *petty*. What does this mean?
  6. When a person has a *grim* expression on his or her face, how does that person look?

Structures

A **Example** It was not necessary for Oppie to drop his old friends.
  Oppie **did not find it necessary** to drop his old friends.

  1. It was not shocking for Chevalier to ask such a question.
  2. It was not pleasant for Oppie to be always suspected.
  3. It was not easy for him to deal with the security men.

4. It was not distressing for the scientists to work in a hot, remote place.
5. But it was not pleasant for their wives to live without comfort.
6. It was not an easy task for Oppie to persuade them to stay.

B *Add all the necessary punctuation to the following text.*

J Robert Oppenheimer who died in 1967 was born in New York in 1904 His father a German Jew had immigrated to the United States in his teens and his mother who incidentally was a painter came from Philadelphia Oppenheimer is now remembered as the father of the atom bomb a title he disliked because it was too oversimplified besides he was not entirely proud of the child Oppenheimer was a man of exceptional intellect and immense curiosity who was interested in just about everything the arts the sciences history philosophy literature languages and sports Although he was prevented from playing tennis because he lacked coordination he could practice the two sports he loved most sailing and horseback riding He deeply enjoyed his modern paintings inherited from his father he also enjoyed music and particularly chamber music Mozart was one of his favorite composers Many of his students became interested in things that they would not have otherwise considered only because of his interest in them But his very superiority and the odd fascination he exerted on people brought him many enemies.

Topics for Discussion or Written Assignment

1. After the Chevalier incident do you blame Oppenheimer for remaining a friend of a communist, or near-communist, after he became director of a very sensitive project like the Manhattan District? Is he to be blamed for his behavior after his conversation with Chevalier? Were General Groves and Colonel Landsdale to be blamed for their indulgence?
2. The United States has welcomed many foreign scientists and has often given them important work, without consideration for their nationality or their past: Albert Einstein, Enrico Fermi, Wernher von Braun, and Edward Teller are examples. Do you approve or disapprove of such policy and why?
3. What do you think of the relationship between Oppenheimer and his students? Have you seen that kind of relationship anywhere between young people and an older person in any walk of life? Would you like to be part of it? Do you think that it is good or bad in the formation of young people?

Questions

1. What was the attitude of the Los Alamos scientists after the explosion of their bomb?
2. What was Oppenheimer's solution?
3. What alternative did the State Department committee and Oppenheimer offer?
4. Why was the Atomic Energy Commission created?
5. How did the sale of radium isotopes to Norway turn Lewis Strauss against Oppenheimer?
6. Who was the champion of the hydrogen bomb?
7. What objections did Oppenheimer have to the hydrogen bomb before 1951?
8. What objections did he have after 1951?
9. What effect did the explosion of the first Russian hydrogen bomb have on William Borden?
10. What was Oppenheimer accused of?
11. What part did Edward Teller play in Oppenheimer's trial?
12. How did the press react to the verdict against Oppenheimer?
13. Who and what have been called responsible for Oppenheimer's trial?
14. What happened to him after the trial?
15. What seems to indicate that Oppenheimer deeply loved his country?

Vocabulary

A *Repeat the following sentences, replacing the word or phrase in italics with one with similar meaning taken from the list.*

hinder	defect
villain	beneficial
promote	diverse
shabby	cast
dreadful	damning
relish	venture
disregard	resume
verdict	farce
bleak	decline

1. Oppenheimer did not join his colleagues' campaign because he had his own idea to *push*.
2. He hoped that research could be done on the *helpful* applications of nuclear energy.
3. In 1950 the future looked *cold and unattractive*. (one word)
4. Oppenheimer found the thermonuclear bomb interesting technically, but he *refused* to work on it.
5. He had *various* objections to the hydrogen bomb.
6. He had tried to *make difficult* the building of the bomb, they said.
7. And this was *throwing* doubts on his patriotism.
8. Teller's remark weighed heavily on the final *decision of the tribunal*.
9. Many people called the hearing a *ridiculous joke*.
10. Oppenheimer had *greatly enjoyed* his power.

B *Repeat the following sentences, filling the blanks with the noun suggested by the verb or adjective in italics.*

1. Oppenheimer was *chairing* many committees, but he was not the _____ of the State Department committee.
2. Lewis Strauss was known to be *vindictive*, and many columnists thought that Oppenheimer's downfall was due to his _____.
3. Oppenheimer had hoped that the United States and the Soviet Union would *agree* to renounce the atom bomb, but they never reached an _____.
4. The security men wanted Oppenheimer *to be dismissed* from the Manhattan project, but General Groves did not accept his _____.
5. Oppenheimer often hurt and *humiliated* people; and Strauss, for one, never forgave him for his public _____.

6. The formation of an international authority was *proposed* at a session of the United Nations Atomic Energy Commission, but the _____ collapsed under Russian opposition.

C *What is:*

1. a catalyst?
2. a radium isotope?
3. a kangaroo court?
4. the Inquisition?

Structure

Example Oppenheimer requested a security hearing.
Oppenheimer **had no choice but to request** a security hearing.

1. The President suspended his clearance.
2. Oppenheimer resigned from his position.
3. They went ahead with the hearing.
4. Oppenheimer answered all questions about his private life.
5. He accepted the verdict.
6. He devoted the rest of his life to the Institute for Advanced Study.

Topics for Discussion or Written Assignment

1. How can physics be a good way "to do philosophy"? Is it a good way toward religion or might it lead away from it? Why?
2. When scientists make discoveries leading to dangerous phenomena or weapons, what should they do? Refuse to go on with the research? Band together and hide the discoveries, knowing that they might sometime lead to beneficial uses as well? Give the results to their government only? Tell the world? Do you understand why pacifist scientists might have worked enthusiastically for the Manhattan project?
3. Do you think that Oppenheimer's trial was justified? On what basis? Because he had kept "dangerous" friends? Because he had been inclined toward communism almost twenty years before? Because he had lied in the Chevalier incident? Because he trusted his judgment about the loyalty of the former communists he hired, rather than the security rules? Because he was not thinking as much in terms of humanity as in terms of his own country? Because he had refused (for what possible reasons?) to work on the hydrogen bomb? Do you approve of the verdict? Do you approve of Edward Teller's answer?
4. What is your final impression of Robert Oppenheimer?

Norman
Mailer

Born January 31, 1923
In Long Branch, New Jersey

There is something larger than life about Norman Mailer. His energy, his imagination, his gifts, and his faults all seem to have heroic proportions. So do his ambitions, which he described in 1959 as "nothing less than making a revolution in the consciousness of our time." This he has done. He has often succeeded in shaking his readers and in putting disturbing questions in their minds. He was one of the first to denounce the role of the United States in Vietnam, for example. His novels and essays° have probed boldly into the diseases of modern society—conformism, mediocrity, alienation,° erotism,° or crime. With his reporting he has inspired a new school of journalism; when Mailer covers a political convention or the launching of Apollo XI the events, the men, and even the rockets take on the dimensions of epic myths.

> short, personal pieces of writing
> feeling of not belonging / continuous thinking of sex

Yet Mailer's defects—his self-absorption,° his stormy and controversial private life, his wild speeches—have sometimes angered even those who were fascinated by his intelligence. Even a loyal admirer can lose patience now and then and mutter that the Great Author is nothing but a conceited, foul-mouthed,° sex-obsessed madman, and that maybe some critics are right when they affirm that he is finished. He once said himself that too much sex, liquor, and drugs had given his brains the texture° of Swiss cheese, didn't he? Perhaps. But it is far from certain. He is now writing an ambitious book, and who knows if it will not be his best one? It just might. It would not be the first time that Mailer has bounced back from the ropes.[1]

> exaggerated concern with oneself
> using dirty language
> structure or appearance

In Mailer's case, the metaphor° could be taken literally,° because he has always loved boxing and was a pretty good boxer himself until a detached retina° forced him to give up his favorite sport. He took up sailing instead. He has also done some gliding, in his own rough and reckless fashion. Rough and reckless—that is Mailer's public image, and it is difficult to decide how much of it is genuine. His friends find him unpredictable° but generous, understanding, and shy. With his sparkling blue eyes, his warmth, his wit, and his gentle

> figure of speech in which one thing is called another / strictly as stated
> lining of the eye
> here, capable of unexpected actions

[1]In boxing, when a fighter has been driven back to the ropes surrounding the arena, he may return to the fight by rebounding from the ropes; here, to recover after almost certain defeat.

manners he can display considerable charm when he chooses. But there is another Mailer—free-drinking and quarrelsome—who has battled with friends, enemies, policemen, and wives. "I like to marry women whom I can beat once in a while and who fight back," he explains. "All my wives have been very good fighters." Four of his five marriages, however, have ended in divorce. He now lives in Brooklyn, where he grew up, with wife number five and the youngest of his seven children, to whom he is a most enthusiastic father. The apartment overlooks the river and a broad expanse of Manhattan skyline. This is the kind of wide open view that he feels is beneficial to his work; it does not break the flight of his inspiration.

Norman Mailer leaped° into fame in 1948 with his first novel, *The Naked and the Dead.* The story centered on a group of officers and enlisted men° occupying a Pacific island during the Second World War and, through them, exposed the character of the Army and of the society that had shaped them. It was both brutal and brilliant; despite its raw° language it met with immediate and overwhelming success. It was justly hailed° as the best novel to come out of the war, and its author was called the new young master of American letters. Mailer, who had not expected such triumph, had some difficulty adjusting to instant fame. "I was blasted a considerable distance away from dead center° by the size of my success," he recalls in his autobiographical *Advertisements for Myself,* "and I spent the next few years trying to swallow the experience of a victorious man when I was still no man at all and had no real gift for enjoying life."

It has been suggested that the triumph of *The Naked and the Dead* also snuffed out° whatever small spark of humility Mailer may have possessed. His egomania° is the subject of innumerable jokes, and pained critics shake their heads over the self-admiration, the self-promotion, and "the compulsive self-analysis" of his writings. Who else would entitle a fat book *Advertisements for Myself?* It's pure Mailer. But nothing is simple in him, not even his famed narcissism.° He has often cautioned his readers not to take everything he says too literally, not to understand him too fast—indeed, not to understand anybody too fast. If he obviously enjoys watching and displaying himself, much of the posturing° and watching is done with irony and with a hint of uncertainty. Nobody casts a more sarcastic eye on Norman Mailer than Norman Mailer

Margin glosses:
- jumped
- soldiers of ranks lower than those of officers
- here, rough, crude
- welcomed
- away . . . off balance
- put out (a light, a fire)
- enormous interest in oneself
- self-love
- taking attitudes for effect

himself; no one pricks° his vanity with more relish; and few other authors, finally, judge themselves with Mailer's total honesty. **sticks with a sharp point**

"I started as a very spoiled boy," he writes in *Advertisements for Myself.* As the only son, bright and likable, of a comfortable family, he had every chance to be spoiled. He was popular at school; he never received a mediocre grade; and Harvard University welcomed him when, at sixteen, he set forth to become an aeronautical engineer. He would surely have made a daring builder. In a room of his Brooklyn apartment stands a large construction that looks like some Disneyland fantasy. It is Mailer's conception of a city of the future—a mammoth° that would be half a mile high, three-quarters of a mile long, and capable of housing 40,000 people. Thus would be solved the problem of coping° with the huge urban population of the twenty-first century without destroying what is left of nature. With its multicolored "houses" suspended from concrete bridges and pylons,° its decks, its zigzags,° its flamboyant explosion of turrets, spires, and minarets,° it would also save the future generations from the uniformity and the boredom of modern architecture. Mailer hates the lack of individuality of our "Kleenex-box" buildings as much as he hates the lack of individuality of the people who inhabit them.

enormous beast (or thing, as here)

dealing successfully

tall towers / series of sharp angles

turrets . . . different types of tall thin towers

When Norman Mailer entered Harvard, he had almost forgotten his first literary venture, a science fiction novel that he had produced at the ripe age of seven. High adventure was his bag° then. He had read and reread all the works of Jeffrey Farnol (*Adam Penfeather, Buccaneer,* and such) and those of Rafael Sabatini, the author of *Captain Blood.* Never in his whole life, says Mailer today, has he enjoyed a novel as much as *Captain Blood,* a rip-roaring° pirate story. He considers it one of the three most important books in his development, the other two being *The Amateur Gentleman,* by Farnol, and Karl Marx's *Capital.*

what he liked most (slang)

very lively, violent

Mailer's future was decided when, in his freshman year, he began to read the great American moderns: Farrell, Dos Passos, Steinbeck, Fitzgerald, Wolfe, Faulkner, and Hemingway. Fired by his discovery of "real" literature and by the sudden realization that significant books could be drawn out of ordinary lives like his own, young Mailer set to work. He wrote copiously,° although not better than his fellow students at first. It is not easy, he found out, to invent a good story: "It is

in great abundance

not easy, when one is young, shy, half in love and certainly self-beloved, sex-ridden yet still weeding out° the acne,° to conceive of oneself (and write about) a hero who is tall, strong, and excruciatingly° wounded." Despite his lack of first-hand experience to feed his prose, Mailer did well enough in his second year to have his stories printed in the Harvard *Advocate* and to win the *Story* magazine College Contest in 1943. He left the university in 1943 with a bachelor's degree in engineering, still writing abundantly.

The Second World War interrupted these literary exercises, but it provided the struggling author with all the experience he needed, and a rich field of observation among the American GI's in combat. Long before setting foot on the troop carrier that was to take him to the Pacific theater of operations, Mailer had determined that he would bring a book back from his adventures. No sooner had he been returned to civilian life, in the spring of 1946, than he sat down and proceeded to disgorge° his booty° in the flowing, surprisingly masterful *The Naked and the Dead.* One can say in retrospect that he did well to enjoy his triumph for all it was worth, because he was never again to hear such a unanimous concert of praise. His second novel, *Barbary Shore,* a murky° mixture of sex and politics, failed miserably. The third one, a strong and depressing study of Hollywood figures called *The Deer Park,* was received more kindly but not triumphantly enough to restore the author's pride. Mailer still considers it the best of all his novels, including the more recent ones, *An American Dream* and *Why Are We in Vietnam?* both of which were shot down in flames° by the critics. Some librarians refused to put *Why Are We in Vietnam?* on their shelves, mostly because of its language. It is definitely not a book for the fainthearted. But what novel of Mailer's is?

II

While waiting for *The Deer Park* to come off the press in 1955, Mailer turned journalist. He had already written many articles for magazines like *Esquire, Dissent, Commentary,* and the *Architectural Forum.* But in 1955 he joined forces with two of his friends to create a weekly newspaper that he named the *Village Voice.* Almost from the beginning the partners found themselves at cross purposes.° "They wanted the paper to be successful," says Mailer. "I wanted it to be outrageous."° Since he was in charge of the editorial column, he did have a chance to outrage the readers to his heart's content. His first article was a declaration of war on "American journalism, mass communication and the totalitarianism of totally pleasant personality." For about six months he managed to make himself totally unpleasant—and outrageous—on a variety of subjects, such as Mailer's intellectual superiority, marijuana, Ed Sullivan,° truth and lies, Dorothy Kilgallen,° the hipsters, the squares, and the reasons why Ernest Hemingway would make a perfect candidate for the presidency against Dwight D. Eisenhower.

After six months and a deluge of spirited letters from readers—some of whom actually liked him—Mailer quit the *Voice* as a columnist, although he remained co-owner of the paper. A change of pace seemed most advisable; he went to France to catch his breath and to get rid of a few bad habits, mostly Benzedrine° and Seconal.° On his return to the United States, he bought a country house and secluded himself in order to meditate° on totalitarianism and on the tragic situation of the modern American. These were themes° that he had been pursuing for several years, and he was eager to explain his philosophy through his works. The simple realistic approach of *The Naked and the Dead* now appeared too superficial to him. He intended to launch into a deeper exploration of the condition of man or, as he put it, "into the mysteries of murder, suicide, incest,° orgy, orgasm,° and Time." *Barbary Shore* had been a first experiment in that direction; hence his distress at its failure.

But what does Mailer call "totalitarianism"? He describes as totalitarian anything and everything that forces or lulls° men into a slick,° saccharin°-sweet conformity, anything that "kills the intellect and dulls man." The government is totalitarian, and so are the FBI, the churches, and the pacifists;° *Time* magazine and the media° in general; modern medicine and its pills; Sigmund Freud and perhaps even Albert Schweitzer. "Totalitarianism sits in the image of the commercials on televison. . . . It is heard in the jargon° of the educators, it resides in the taste of frozen food, the pharmaceutical° odor of tranquilizers,° the lack of workmanship° of the masses; it lives in the boredom of a good mind and it proliferates° in that new architecture which cannot be called modern architecture

Marginal glosses:
- at . . . opposed to each other
- shocking
- famous columnist and television personality / columnist of the 1950s and 1960s
- a stimulant drug / a depressant drug
- think seriously
- topics, subjects
- sexual relations between members of the same family / sexual climax
- quiets down
- smooth and slippery / chemical sweeter than sugar
- people opposed to war
- radio, televison, and newspapers
- technical language
- of drugs
- drugs that calm / quality of work
- multiplies

because it is not architecture. . . . The essence of totalitarianism is that it beheads.° It beheads individuality, variety, °cuts off heads
dissent,° extreme possibility, romantic faith; it blinds vision, °different opinions
deadens instinct, obliterates° the past." °removes, erases

Most men, says Mailer, drown in totalitarianism without ever knowing it. But as their unconscious urges conflict with the values imposed on them by a brainwashed society, they suffer from a hopeless schizophrenia.° Incidentally, they also contract °severe personality disorder
cancer, a disease that, according to Mailer, is caused by all the things that a man has failed to feel and do. Modern America, Mailer repeats darkly, is schizophrenic.

Since there are no more adventurers, no more bold pioneers, no more revolutionaries in North America today, Mailer's sympathy goes to the only independent souls he can see: the hipsters. To them he has devoted a controversial essay, "The White Negro." The hipster is a rebel, voluntarily divorced from a society that has nothing to offer him but a violent death in some insane war or a slow one from living in suffocating° °smothering
conformity. He has chosen instead to live only in the present, "the enormous present," and exclusively for himself. The hipster has no other goal in life than to explore human nature in his own person through the widest possible range of experiences, whether with drugs, sex, jazz, mysticism, violence, or anything else that might heighten his awareness. Mailer has denied being hip himself, but like the hipsters he has been trying to get more experience, more expression, and to dig deeper "into the nuances° of things." He sees his °slight variations
philosophy as an American existentialism "based on the mysticism of the flesh," and very different from the French existentialism, which is too intellectual and rational for his taste.

While he was cherishing° the idea of being "the first °fondly thinking of
philosopher of Hip," Mailer had been relying heavily on drugs to widen his field of exploration. The combination of alcohol, drugs, and personal frustrations caught up with him in 1960. Early one morning, after a rowdy° party and some fist fights, he °rough and noisy
walked sullenly to his wife and stabbed her several times with a knife, missing her heart by sheer luck. The episode° earned °incident, event
him a period of observation in a mental institution and plenty of disastrous publicity—not to mention his second divorce. It also ruined his chances of becoming mayor of New York City in 1961.

The pen is a mighty weapon, and Mailer does not

underestimate it. "The writer affects the consciousness of his time," he once said in an interview, "and so indirectly he affects the history of the time which succeeds him." But all this takes time and patience, and Mailer is no more patient than any other energetic and ambitious man. He wrote half seriously in 1959 that for years he had been running for president in the privacy of his own mind. In 1960 he chose more realistically to run for mayor of New York, as an "existential" candidate. The stabbing of his wife ruined any chances he may have had, but he could not give up the idea. In 1969 he entered the mayoral primaries[2] as a Democrat. He was well aware that a political career would involve some sacrifice, since he would not have much time for writing if elected. But then he would have his hand "on the rump° of history," an idea he found most appealing. hind part, rear end

He campaigned with determination. Unfortunately, New Yorkers were unimpressed by his ideas of legalizing gambling at Coney Island and of making New York City the fifty-first state of the Union. Neither did they like his proposal of fighting air pollution by having a "Sweet Sunday" every month, during which all forms of mechanical transportation would be forbidden, including elevators. When the time came to vote, they did worse than defeat him, they practically ignored him.

Mailer ventured into another alien° field in the 1960s. He foreign turned to moviemaking. With his friends as actors and no script performance without preparation / to hinder his improvisation,° he directed three wild° films, one here, unruly, unrestrained about the Mafia° (Wild 90), one about the police (Beyond the secret criminal organization Law), and one about Mailer's own presidential aspirations, (Maidstone). They were obscure,° to put it mildly, and ugly not clear comments were heard from the critics. But, wrote one, if the ordeal° of sitting through this is the price one has to pay for very painful experience having Mailer write in one year The Armies of the Night and Miami and the Siege of Chicago, then it is worth it.

Besides his novels, Mailer has written many essays, collected in The White Negro, Cannibals and Christians, The Idol and the Octopus, and The Presidential Papers. He has also written several books on political or historical events: Of a Fire on the Moon, about the launching of Apollo XI; Miami and the Siege of Chicago, his coverage of the Republican and Democratic presidential conventions of 1968; Saint George and the

[2]Elections held before the general election, in which the members of each party choose their candidate to run in the general election.

Norman Mailer directing the actors in his film Maidstone, *in Southampton, New York, 1968.*

Godfather, about the conventions of 1972; and *The Armies of the Night,* an account of the anti-Vietnam War demonstration at the Pentagon in 1967 and Mailer's participation in the march, his arrest, and his two days in jail. There may be too much Mailer in the foreground,° but even this could not prevent *The Armies of the Night* from being a remarkable epic. It received the Pulitzer Prize[3] in 1968, while *Miami and the Siege of Chicago* won the National Book Award granted by the publishing industry (publishers and booksellers). Thus was the seal° of approval stamped on Mailer's unique brand of

° the closest part of a picture

° official mark

[3]A yearly award for outstanding work in American journalism, fiction, music, and art.

journalism, an articulate° mixture of facts and wild theories, clearly arranged and expressed
sharp portraits, keen judgments, and "existential" philosophy,
all flowing on Mailer's exuberant° prose. It is also completely full of life
subjective;° but why bother about objectivity,° since "truth is coming from the mind of the viewer alone / reality independent from the viewer
no more or less than what one feels at each instant in the
perpetual climate of the present"?

Mailer's severest critics have often expressed regret that he
should waste his talent on what they consider weak books,
such as *The Prisoner of Sex*, his answer to the attacks on him by
women's lib, for whom he is the worst male chauvinist° of them male . . . man who believes that men are superior to women
all, or *Marilyn*, his "biography" of Marilyn Monroe, based
completely on previously published books and articles (he
never met her). One can also regret Mailer's uninhibited
behavior when he is in his cups.° But for all his faults, Norman drunk
Mailer is a splendidly gifted writer, a perceptive and
provocative° commentator of contemporary America and of stimulating, causing discussion
man's fate. His courage at least cannot be denied. Mailer does
not mind being discussed and denounced as long as he can
bring some useful ideas to the minds of his readers. The role of
the artist, as he sees it, is precisely to be disturbing, alive, "as
adventurous, as penetrating as his energy and courage make
possible." He would rather act than write, but "it's no little
matter to be a writer. There is that awful *Time* magazine world
out there. There are palaces and prisons to attack. . . . There
is something rich waiting if one of us is brave enough and good
enough to get there." Mailer is now hard at work on an
enormous novel, for which he has already a contract for one
million dollars, and which, he hopes, will be the great
achievement of his life.

Questions

1. What seems to be the general subject of Mailer's books?
2. Does he seem to be a mediocre man? Why?
3. Why is it fitting to describe him as "bouncing back from the ropes"?
4. What book made him famous, and what was it about?
5. Why do critics joke about Mailer?
6. Why does he dislike modern architecture?
7. What solution does he have for the housing problem?
8. What novels of Mailer's can you name?
9. Have they all failed?
10. Why did some librarians object to *Why Are We in Vietnam?*

Vocabulary

A 1. What is the retina?
2. a metaphor?
3. a zigzag?
4. a pylon?
5. a mammoth?
6. narcissism?
7. an essay?

B 1. If you say that your best friend is *unpredictable,* what does that mean?
2. How would you describe the *texture* of Swiss cheese?
3. How would you *prick* a balloon?
4. What is an *outrageous* remark?
5. If you help yourself *copiously* to cake, does it mean that you are taking a very small or very large piece?
6. What does an *egomaniac* do?
7. What do a *turret,* a *spire,* and a *minaret* have in common?
8. What *metaphor* is used to say that the critics strongly condemned Mailer's novels *An American Dream* and *Why Are We in Vietnam?*

Structures

A **Example** He cautions his readers, "Don't understand me too fast."
He cautions his readers **not to understand him too fast.**

1. His friends tell us, "Don't believe everything you hear about Mailer."
2. He tells them, "Don't take the story too literally."
3. The librarian advised me, "Don't read Mailer's new novel."
4. She told us, "Don't put that book back on the shelf."
5. The editor advised him, "Don't use such raw language in your article."
6. Mailer cautions us, "Don't destroy what is left of nature."

B **Example** Perhaps it will be his best one.
Who knows if it will not be his best one?

1. Perhaps he is right.
2. Perhaps his brains are made of Swiss cheese.
3. Perhaps he is as reckless as they say.
4. Perhaps he will marry again.
5. Perhaps his wife likes to be beaten.
6. Perhaps he would have been an excellent engineer.
7. Perhaps his city-of-the-future will be built.
8. Perhaps it will be fun to live in it.

Topics for Discussion or Written Assignment

1. A librarian refused to put *Why Are We in Vietnam?* on the shelf of a public library because she found the language and parts of the story very shocking. Was she right? Should all books without exception be put on the shelves of a public library? Should there be any control of books, films, plays, and television shows? To what extent? How?
2. When you have children, will you let them read and see anything they want? Justify your answer.
3. What does Mailer mean when he says, "Don't understand anybody too fast"?
4. What kind of books would you like to write, and why?
5. Have you ever decided not to read a book, see a movie, or buy a record because you did not like something in the personality, the private life, or the political ideas of the author, the actor, or the singer? Are such factors important in the success of an artist? Give examples. Are they important in other lines of activity?
6. Is self-analysis good or bad? Explain your answer.

Questions

1. What is the *Village Voice?*
2. What do you know about Mailer's columns in it?
3. What were the readers' reactions?
4. Why did he stop writing books like *The Naked and the Dead?*
5. Do you understand what Mailer considers totalitarian?
6. What would you add to his list?
7. Why does Mailer like the hipsters?
8. What can you say about Mailer's moviemaking?
9. What did Mailer plan to do as mayor of New York?
10. How does Mailer see the role of a writer?

Vocabulary

A   *Choose the most accurate of the three words or phrases.*

1. Jargon
    a) technical language
    b) dispute
    c) foreigner

2. Rowdy
    a) rough
    b) new
    c) in bad condition

3. Episode
    a) knifing
    b) long novel
    c) an incident

4. Foreground
    a) the upper part of the face
    b) the back of the head
    c) the closest part of a picture

5. Objectivity
    a) personal view
    b) real view
    c) goal

6. To proliferate
   a) to multiply
   b) to modify
   c) to replace with

B *Repeat the following sentences, replacing the word or phrase in italics with one with similar meaning taken from the list.*

uninhibited	lull
cherish	outrageous
incest	articulate
reside	behead
dissent	obscure
proliferate	ordeal
hinder	indulge in

1. Totalitarianism, says Mailer, *puts* men *to sleep.*
2. It also *cuts off their heads.*
3. It kills individuality, variety, and *difference of opinion.*
4. Watching Mailer's movies, said a critic, was a *painful experience.*
5. Mailer *thinks fondly of* the idea of being the philosopher of hip.
6. Totalitarianism has not dulled him; he is still completely *unrestrained.*
7. In the 1960s he *gave himself the pleasure of* moviemaking.
8. His films were wild and *not very clear,* to put it mildly.

Structures

A **Example** He received letters from his readers; some readers actually liked him.
He received letters from his readers, **some of whom** actually liked him.

1. He had five wives; one wife was a beautiful South American artist.
2. He had seven children; four children live with him in Brooklyn.
3. He was arrested with a group of demonstrators; most of the demonstrators did not know him.
4. He has a large number of friends; all his friends find him generous and understanding.
5. He has written about several famous figures; the last figure was Marilyn Monroe.

B **Example** They did not like his idea of legalizing gambling. And they did not like his other proposals either.
Neither did they like his other proposals.

1. Mailer has not forgotten *Captain Blood.* He has not forgotten Farnol's *Amateur Gentleman* either.
2. He was not the worst student of his English class. He was not the best one either.
3. He was not elected President of the United States. He was not elected mayor of New York either.
4. The critics did not like *An American Dream.* They did not like *Why Are We in Vietnam?* either.
5. Mailer is not a hipster. He is not a square either.
6. Most readers did not like his ideas. They did not like his uninhibited style either.

Topics for Discussion or Written Assignment

1. What is your overall impression of Norman Mailer? Do you like or dislike him and why?
2. Who are the hipsters? Can you think of people, artists, and actors who are or represent hipsters? What do you think of the hipsters? Do you admire them, envy them, pity them?
3. Do you consider yourself objective or subjective? Justify your answer. Can you think of an author, a journalist, a politician, or any other person you know who seems to be objective? Are journalists usually objective or subjective? Defend your answer. *Should* a writer be objective? An artist?
4. What do you think of Mailer's "Sweet Sunday" idea? Of legalizing gambling? Should marijuana be legalized? Should all drugs be legalized?
5. Do you agree with Mailer's definition of truth?

Andrew
Wyeth

Born July 12, 1917
In Chadds Ford, Pennsylvania

"What Wyeth does is all right, if you like that sort of thing," sniffed° the director of a modern art gallery a few years ago. "But he is not important, he is not influential; he is not avant-garde.° *He does what has been done before.*" Horrors! And so he does, in his very personal way. Distant and obviously undismayed,° Wyeth goes on polishing his own kind of pictures in the peace and privacy of what is now called "Wyeth's country," a modest county of Pennsylvania and a small stretch of coastal Maine. The only aspect of his art that could be considered daring° is that, in an era of artistic shocks and experiments, it remains firmly traditional. Such as it is, its effect on the public has been astonishing. Wyeth is probably the best known American painter today, and by far the most popular. Not only does he sell whatever he cares to offer at eyebrow-raising° prices, but any exhibition of his works draws crowds of visitors, many of whom will come several times. Let a large museum in New York, Buffalo, Philadelphia, San Francisco, or anywhere else organize a Wyeth show, and tens of thousands of people will rush to it, resigned to walking from distant parking places, to standing in line at the door, and to waiting their turn once inside, for a chance to see the paintings. They look at them long and close. They stare at the unbelievable details—the hair you can almost touch, the blades of grass, the grain of a fabric, the lace of a delicate curtain swelled by the sea breeze. "I don't know why it gets to me° so much," said a visitor to a recent Wyeth exhibition in San Francisco. "He seems to say something about the United States that nobody else can quite put their finger on." And another one added, "This is my third visit. I'll come again. It disturbs me but I have to come back."

Wyeth's following among connoisseurs and nonconnoisseurs alike makes one wonder about the nature of his appeal. It has been suggested that most people admire him for the wrong reason: they are fascinated and misled° by his meticulous° realism. Wyeth, who describes himself as an abstractionist,[1] affirms that his audience, although attracted first by the photographic precision of his pictures, learns to perceive and

[1]Painter whose work does not represent real persons or objects.

here, said with contempt

ahead of the times

unmoved, not upset

bold

surprising

it moves me

led to error/ extremely careful

appreciate the abstraction. He likes to look at his own pictures in the dark, where shapes and colors lose their meaning. But who else does? One of his first watercolors, he recalls happily, was hung upside down once. There is little chance of the accident being repeated, even with his barest landscapes, such as *Hoffman's Slough,*° which could be mistaken from a distance for an arrangement of brownish triangles edged in white. _{swamp, water-filled ground}

Whatever charms Wyeth's admirers, it cannot be the variety or the cheerfulness of his colors. He restricts himself to browns, tans, creamy whites, and rich greens, rarely relieved by a touch of red, or perhaps a faded blue. It comes as a surprise, in his famous *Christina's World,* to find Christina wearing a pink dress. But there she is, dragging her crippled° body toward her house through an open field. Christina Olson, a victim of polio,[2] was a neighbor of Wyeth's in Cushing, Maine, and one of his favorite models. He saw her in that field one day. "I looked at her, this marvelous, strange shade of pink she had; it looked like one of those lobster shells dried out on a New England beach. . . . I felt the loneliness of that figure, perhaps the way I felt myself as a kid. So it's as much an experience of mine as it was hers, do you see? That's the point. After all, you are expressing your own emotions. I start every painting with an emotion."

And this is probably what catches most of Wyeth's fans, what brings tears to the eyes of a visitor, for example, in front of a simple picture of an open window. A Wyeth painting is a loaded painting; it is heavy with hidden meaning. Whether the painter's original emotion is obvious or not, his work puzzles and suggests enough to start viewers' imaginations working. They try to read between the lines, so to speak, and from their personal experience they supply stories, usually sad ones, for Wyeth's pictures speak of loneliness, decay, and defeat. His landscapes° are fall or winter scenes—damp brown earth, dead leaves, patches of snow, pale sun. A heavy mood also hangs about his portraits and about the forlorn°-looking objects of his still lifes,° which in a way are portraits too. Wyeth makes no distinction between his subjects, animate° or inanimate. To him they are all signs, they are all symbols. The boat, high and dry in the grass in *Teel's Island,* is a symbol of seafaring° Maine; it also symbolizes Wyeth's friend Henry Teel, a lobsterman who pulled the boat aground before taking to his

_{lame, twisted by disease or injury}

_{pictures of natural scenery}

_{sad, lonely}
_{pictures of fruit, flowers, and household objects}
_{living}

_{making a living from the sea}

[2]Poliomyelitis, a disease that often cripples its victims.

bed to die. It also stands for Wyeth himself, mourning. Behind the gloomy hill of *Winter 1946*, where a small boy runs as if in flight, Wyeth's father was killed in an automobile accident. "I was sick I had never painted him. The boy is really me, at a loss;° the hand drifting in the air is my free soul, grop-ing.° . . . The hill to me became finally a portrait of my father."

at . . . not knowing what to do

trying to find by reaching out

Going to an Andrew Wyeth exhibit after the first time is like revisiting old friends. Again and again you run into the familiar faces. In this picture are Karl Kuerner and his farm in

Andrew Wyeth, Christina's World *(1948). Tempera on gesso panel, 32¼″ × 47¾″. Collection, The Museum of Modern Art.*

Chadds Ford; here are the Olsons from Cushing; here is Betty Wyeth under a Quaker hat or asleep in the grass. Here is young Siri Erickson in a series of very innocent nudes. And here is Willard Snowden, *The Drifter,* a black merchant seaman who appeared in Chadds Ford one day, after traveling the world, and settled in a room above Wyeth's studio. Bemused° by his eloquence, his elegant manners, and his air of mystery, the artist painted him many times. Like Christina, Snowden makes a compelling model. And so does Karl Kuerner, glaring

surprised, confused

malevolently° at the viewer under a low ceiling that bears two with evil intent
ominous° meat hooks. We may not know—if we have not read threatening
Wyeth's accompanying commentary—that Karl is listening for
his demented° wife downstairs; but we cannot doubt that we mad, insane
are looking at a tragic figure. Wyeth's models seldom face him
and the public as Karl does. With their eyes closed or downcast
in private sorrow, or with their backs turned, or staring into the
distance, they give an impression of despair and loneliness, the
same loneliness that pervades° Wyeth's bare interiors, his fills
abandoned objects, his brown hills with roads "which seem to
lead to mysterious places."

Wyeth sees all of his models through kind and reverent eyes.
Old Tom Clark asleep in his garret is *That Gentleman*, Willard
Snowden is "a Mongol° prince," and Nordic° Walt Anderson, tribe of Northeastern Asia/
from Scandinavia (Norway,
Sweden, and so on)
the Maine fisherman, was "a young princeling" when Wyeth
made his first portrait of him. As for the formidable Christina,
who would impress less sympathetic people as a witch with
her fierce look, her Medusa[3] hair, and her crooked° limbs, to deformed, not straight
her admirer Wyeth she is royalty. "My God, that fabulous
person! She is everybody's conscience. You see before you the
power of the Queen of Sweden, looking at you. . . . She rules
like a Queen, absolutely." Even Ralph Cline, the owner of a
sawmill in Cushing, who sat for one of Wyeth's most delightful
portraits *(The Patriot),* is "a baron° in a bib° overall." Wyeth a nobleman/
flap that covers the chest
painted Cline in his old First World War uniform and medals,
smiling in Mona Lisa[4] fashion at secret memories of the
Argonne battle—lost buddies, brave deeds or escapades,° who adventures
knows? Ralph Cline is the incarnation° of the First World War representation in bodily
form
stories that Andrew used to read, spellbound,° in his father's fascinated
collection of yellowed newspapers when he was a boy. But
Ralph is also Maine and Maine's strong trees, and he is the
spirit of America. "Kind of man who fought at Concord Bridge.
He is every inch the patriot. The American flag means
everything to him."

Chadds Ford, Pennsylvania, and Cushing, Maine—two small
spots in the oldest portion of the United States, once part of the
British colonial empire. This is Andrew Wyeth's territory. Both
states have deep roots in American history and still preserve

[3]In Greek myth, a hideous woman whose head was covered with live snakes.
Her glance turned men to stone.
[4]A famous painting by Leonardo da Vinci, representing a woman with a faint,
mysterious smile.

much of the character and way of life of the colonial society. They cherish their memories and their traditions. Up north on the Atlantic coast, Cushing's scattered houses barely deserve the name "village," and chances are that the 414 permanent residents like it that way. They are independent folk, shrewd,° *having good judgment* a bit on the dour° side perhaps, but not without their share of *stern, severe* dry° humor. They are not unfriendly but notoriously *here, quiet* uncommunicative. They mind their own business and look with suspicion at the inlanders° who at the end of spring *people who live away from the coast* descend on the coast to open their summer cottages. This is precisely what Andrew's parents used to do. He spent all his summers with them at nearby Port Clyde, in a house that had belonged to a sea captain. Young Andrew must have thought of it as a reminder of Maine's shipbuilding days, when the New England states were launching fleets of merchant ships and whaling vessels.° At the end of their careers, the captains *ships used to catch whales* would come back home and build themselves stately houses in which to retire and reminisce.° *recall the past*

If the former owner had appeared on a moonless night in the Wyeth house, it would have delighted Andrew, who had—and still has—a fascination for the supernatural. Ghosts, goblins,° *imaginary creatures, short and mischievous* devils, and witches—he loves them all. Cushing, where he spends part of the year, is located in "witch country," a fact much more stimulating to him than the picturesque seaside resorts or the lovely countryside. Wyeth is not interested in pretty views or sweet pictures. To him nature means suppressed violence and cruelty rather than charm and kindness. He is enchanted with Maine's rough, forthright° *direct* spirit. "It's a clear, clean, remote place, a damask° napkin. I *a heavy, shiny cloth* love Maine because it has an edge—like Ralph Cline."

II

A battle was fought at Chadds Ford during the Revolutionary War. The British surprised George Washington there and roundly° defeated him on the afternoon of September 11, *severely* 1777. Many men died; the wounded had to be left on the field to be taken prisoner; and Washington's friend, the marquis de Lafayette, received a bullet in the leg. It was, all told, a rather gloomy affair—not so gloomy, however, as to distress the hardy° Yankee volunteers, who swore to each other that they *strong and durable* would do better next time, as they retreated to cover Philadelphia. Its hour of glory and disaster gone, Chadds Ford went back to work, as befits a sober village with nothing much to boast about except its rolling hills, its good farms, a Quaker[5] meetinghouse° or two, and a frisky° little river with the most un-Quakerish name of Brandywine.

here, place of worship/ playful

Nowadays Brandywine country (Chester County) is still devoted to farming and tries to protect itself against the encroachments° of Wilmington, a large industrial city whose suburbs are beginning to push into Chadds Ford. The Wyeths play an active part in the residents' efforts to protect it. This part of Pennsylvania had been mostly settled by English immigrants, with some Dutch, Welsh, and Scandinavians. A few Swiss came too, among them Andrew Wyeth's maternal ancestors. A substantial part of the English colony was made up of Quakers, who gave the area a character of frugality° and severity, the very characteristics of Wyeth's painting. Gentle as it is, Chester County seems to have its own touch of devilishness;° some of its honest old houses have rounded windowsills "to keep off the witches." What more did it need to be perfect?

intrusions, advances

strict economy

mischief, wickedness

Wyeth's fondness for the mysterious and the fantastic may well be due to the influence of his father, Newell Convers Wyeth. "N. C.," as he was known, was himself a noted artist, an illustrator of swashbuckling° novels such as *Robin Hood,* Robert Louis Stevenson's *Treasure Island,* and James Fenimore Cooper's Indian stories. His powerful and beautifully composed illustrations conveyed° the romanticism of his nature. He was a giant of a man, flamboyant but sensitive, and endowed with a tremendous love for life. The magic and suspense and glitter° of Christmas made it the most exciting part of the year for him, and he kept it alive long after proper Christmas decorations are usually dismantled.° He turned it into such an experience that the spell still endures, not only for Andrew and his sisters, but for the younger generation represented by Andrew's sons, Nick and Jamie. Andrew remembers that his father, in full Santa Claus regalia,° would climb onto the roof the night before Christmas, jingling bells and thumping his heavy boots, while his five children hid under their blankets in delighted terror. Fear, joy, wonderment

full of romance and daring

expressed

brilliant light

taken down

costume

[5]Member of a religious group (The Society of Friends) devoted to simplicity, direct divine guidance, and the rejection of formal rituals and clergy.

—all emotions and all experiences were welcomed by N. C. as important elements in the formation of his children's minds. "Pa felt that you build a reserve of reflection, a rich background, so that if you are an artist or a writer or a musician or whatever, it gives you more meat in depth. He often said that a person is like a sponge; you soak everything up and wring it out now and then; don't run away from experience. So by God he'd shake the whole roof till our teeth would chatter."

N. C. Wyeth took infinite precautions to let his children develop their own personalities and talents independently of him. One of his gifted daughters is now a composer and the others are painters (one of them is married to the Western artist Peter Hurd). Andrew, the youngest child, was also the weakest. His poor health forced him to leave school after a few months in first grade, and from then on private tutors attempted to conduct his education. But formal learning was never Andrew's cup of tea.° With no pressure on him, he lived pretty much as he pleased "on the edge of the family," roaming° the countryside and dreaming his dreams in solitude.° He is still a loner° who loves nothing better than to walk by himself or to sit in a cornfield on a windy fall day, listening to the dry rustle° of the leaves and feeling "the way a king must have felt walking down the long line of knights on horseback with banners blowing." Wyeth does not allow such heroic visions to invade his canvases,° but his romanticism can nevertheless be felt in the sober, tawny° paintings familiar to his admirers —more powerful perhaps for being forced into the background.

While attempting to show at least some enthusiasm for algebra and English grammar, young Andy was continually drawing and painting, and N. C. soon must have realized that he had a prodigy° on his hands. Andrew made his first illustration for a book when he was twelve; at fifteen he had a watercolor in a show, and his first one-man show in New York, when he was twenty, was a sellout. He was then painting brilliant watercolors that sold well but did not satisfy him. He found them gaudy° and superficial, unworthy of the efforts made by his father to teach him not the "tricks of the trade," but the art of observing the world patiently and lovingly. In an effort to get more depth and to curb° his facility, he decided to work in a different medium:° tempera.

Tempera requires infinite patience because the pigments,° mixed with egg yolk instead of oil or water, have to be prepared

cup . . . . favorite activity

wandering through

in . . . alone

one who avoids other people

soft rubbing sound

cloths on which pictures are painted

yellow-brown

extremely talented child

too colorful

keep under control

here, material used for a painting

coloring elements

and applied to the canvas in very small quantities. "Such a dull medium," sighs Wyeth. It does not allow the spontaneity° of watercolors, but it works perfectly, if slowly, for the kind of exquisitely detailed pictures he produces. Wyeth finishes about two tempera paintings a year, besides a handful of watercolors. He enjoys both media—the watercolors because they take him out of doors and let him show what he calls his "wild" side; the tempera because it disciplines him. The turning point in his career came in 1946 when his father's car collided with a train behind the hill in Chadds Ford. Andrew was so shattered by N. C.'s death that for months he could neither work nor think clearly. Slowly emerged a compulsion "to do something serious, not caricatures° of nature. . . . When he died, I was just a clever watercolorist; now I was really on the spot° and had this terrific urge to prove that what he had started in me was not in vain. Fortunately, I had always felt a great emotion towards the landscape, and so with his death the landscape took a meaning, the quality of him." The first tempera Andrew painted then was *Winter 1946.*

 Since that time, Andrew Wyeth has been following his own course, which is a highly personal one in the sense that he remains indifferent to what happens in contemporary art and that he paints only people and places that have meaning for him. That meaning, as often as not,° remains obscure to the public. The viewers have to read the program or the cards under the pictures to know why Wyeth chose to paint two plain white doors, a gun hanging from a nail, or the back of a man who is looking out a window. But they do react to that elusive° quality that makes his admirers speak of poetry, romanticism, or diabolism,° while his critics counter with "coldness" or "sentimentality."

 The least brooding° of all Wyeth's models is his wife, the former Betsy James, the daughter of a newspaper editor from Buffalo, New York. He met her in Maine in the summer of 1939, when they were both vacationing in their families' summer homes. Everything about seventeen-year-old Betsy attracted young Andrew: her healthy good looks, her black hair, and the simplicity of her life on the James farm, which involved more house-painting and berry-picking than social glitter. Ten months after their first meeting, they were married and already arranging their life around the two now-familiar poles— Chadds Ford and Cushing. In Cushing they have a small

Glosses (right margin):
- freedom, naturalness
- humorous or ironic distortions
- I was . . . I had to prove myself
- as often . . . in many cases
- difficult to understand
- witchcraft
- sad and thoughtful

Andrew Wyeth, Wind from the Sea *(1947). Tempera, 18½" × 27½". Private collection.*

house at the edge of the sea, simple and bare as a Wyeth painting; in Chadds Ford they own an old schoolhouse, where Wyeth paints, and an eighteenth-century mill that must have seen General Washington and the redcoats and that is now their home. Of the Wyeths' two sons, the elder, Nicholas, is an art dealer in New York. "Nicky can sell anything," says the proud father. "Once at school he sold his roommate his own tie." The younger one, Jamie, has been a superb portrait painter since his teens. He made a famous portrait of President Kennedy. He has also surprised the art world by lovingly painting a portrait of his favorite pig. His work is eagerly sought by private collectors and museums, and according to some critics, Jamie will surpass° his father just as Andrew [do better than] surpassed N. C. So goes the Wyeth dynasty.° [here, family succession]

There seems to be no end to the inspiration that Andrew Wyeth finds in his narrow circle—the shells, the sea, the apple trees of his orchard,° and the circle of his old friends in Chadds [field planted with fruit trees] Ford and Cushing. He ventures seldom and reluctantly away from his base, although he did have to go to Washington to paint a portrait of President Eisenhower and later to attend a dinner given in his honor by another President, before a month-long show of his paintings at the White House. Many honors have been lavished° on him: awards from art *given generously* associations, the first Medal for Merit[6] given to an artist, and a number of honorary degrees from universities, which unscholarly Wyeth accepts with amused gratitude. He stays home. "From my first girl friend to great art critics," he smiles, "I have been criticized as being too narrow. They say 'Andrew, it would help your work to travel abroad . . . you'd come back with a fresh eye.' But after you travel, you are never the same. You get more erudite,° you get more knowledge. But I might *learned* lose something very important to my work—perhaps innocence."

[6]Decoration awarded by the United States to civilians for exceptional services.

Exercises for Section I   *pp. 126-130*

Questions

1. Why doesn't the director of the modern art gallery admire Andrew Wyeth?
2. How does the public respond to a Wyeth show?
3. What makes people think of Wyeth's paintings as realistic?
4. What can you say about the colors and the subjects of his paintings?
5. Who is Christina Olson?
6. What made Wyeth paint her when he saw her in her field?
7. Why are viewers moved and often depressed by Wyeth's paintings?
8. What is "Wyeth's country"?
9. What do you know about Cushing, Maine?
10. Why does Wyeth like Maine?

Andrew Wyeth

Vocabulary

A *What is:*

1. an avant-garde artist?
2. a swashbuckling novel?
3. a still life?
4. a landscape?
5. a slough?
6. a goblin?

B *Repeat the following sentences, replacing the word or phrase in italics with one with similar meaning taken from the list.*

bemused	notoriously
roundly	grope
malevolently	forlorn
sniff at me	meticulously
dour	reminisce
ominous	pervade
get at me	misled
forthright	at a loss

1. Wyeth's models always look *sad and lonely.*
2. His paintings always *move me.*
3. The details of his pictures are so *extremely carefully* painted that you think they are real.
4. The death of his father left him *not knowing what to do.*
5. Wyeth was *confused* by the "drifter" Willard Snowden.
6. A feeling of loneliness *fills* his paintings.
7. Kuerner glares *with evil intent* at the public.
8. The meat hooks look *threatening.*
9. Sea captains like *to recall the past.*
10. The people of Maine are very *direct.*

Structures

A **Example** He sells his paintings easily, and his exhibitions draw large crowds.

Not only does he sell his paintings easily, but his exhibitions draw large crowds.

1. He is the best-known American painter, and he is by far the most popular.

2. They wait patiently in line to see his paintings, and they do not mind waiting again another day.
3. The connoisseurs admire him, and the nonconnoisseurs are interested too.
4. They are fascinated by his painstaking realism, and they respond to the heavy mood of his paintings.
5. The boat represents seafaring Maine, and it serves also as a symbol of Wyeth's mourning.
6. He tried to show Christina's loneliness, and he expressed his own emotions at the same time.

B *Repeat the following sentences, replacing the words or phrases in italics with* **whoever** (person), **whatever** (object), **whenever** (time), **wherever** (place).

1. He sells *anything* he cares to offer at *any* price he cares to set.
2. *No matter where* his paintings are shown, they attract huge crowds of faithful admirers.
3. *The man who* said that about him was rather naive.
4. *No matter what* he may say, most people do not see him as an abstractionist.
5. *Any time* he sees Christina Olson she reminds him of absolute power.
6. *Any person who* saw Christina in her kitchen would be reminded of a witch.
7. *Any time* you go to Cushing, try to visit the Wyeth museum.
8. *Any place* he goes in Cushing, he finds people or things to paint.

Topics for Discussion or Written Assignment

1. What kind of picture do you prefer: portraits, still lifes, landscapes, seascapes, abstractions? Beautiful, amusing, or disturbing pictures? Explain your choice.
2. Wyeth says that all his paintings start with an emotion. What do you think starts a work of art (painting, musical composition, statue, or poem)? What can start a book?
3. What does patriotism mean to you? Is it the patriotism of Ralph Cline, to whom "the flag means everything"?
4. Why would anyone cry when looking at a picture of an open window showing nothing but the window, slightly torn curtains blowing in the breeze, a brown lawn, a bit of sea, and dark trees in the distance?

Exercises for Section II pp. 130-135

Questions

1. What happened during that day of "glory and disaster" in Chadds Ford?
2. Is the word *glory* entirely ironical here?
3. What problem does Chadds Ford have to face now?
4. Why is it said that Chester County has everything it needs to be perfect?
5. What kind of person was Andrew Wyeth's father?
6. Why did he scare his children?
7. What impression do you have of Andrew Wyeth's childhood?
8. What kind of paintings was he doing at the beginning of his career?
9. What is tempera painting?
10. In what sense is Wyeth's work personal?
11. How did his father's death change Andrew's work?
12. Are Andrew's sons successful in their careers? Explain.

True or False

If the statement is false, correct it.

1. Wyeth's ancestors were Scandinavian.
2. Andrew's father was very much interested in the development of his children.
3. Andrew did not absorb much formal education.
4. From his father he learned only "the tricks of the trade."
5. Wyeth's critics find him cold.
6. Now that he is so famous, he has to travel a great deal.

Vocabulary

A. *Repeat the following sentences, replacing the blank with the noun suggested by the adjectives or verbs in italics.*

1. Wyeth does not paint *abstract* pictures, but he thinks of himself as an _____ just the same.
2. His subjects are *varied*, but there is not much _____ in his colors.
3. As a child Andrew showed a *prodigious* talent. One of his sons was also a child _____.

4. When he lost his father, Andrew Wyeth felt *compelled* to change his style. He had a _____ to do something more serious than his watercolors.
5. N. C. Wyeth was a very *romantic* artist. Andrew has inherited his _____.
6. All the paintings of his first show were *sold out*. Any show of his works would also be a _____ now, if the pictures were for sale.
7. Wyeth is *grateful* for all the awards lavished on him, but it is with amused _____ that he accepts the honorary degrees offered by universities.
8. N. C. Wyeth *illustrated* popular novels. He was one of the best _____ of his time.

B *Choose the most accurate of the three words or phrases.*

1. Frisky
   a) playful
   b) short
   c) very cold

2. Frugality
   a) excessive severity
   b) a bad disposition
   c) strict economy

3. Dismantle
   a) take apart
   b) undress
   c) reject

4. Tawny
   a) yellow-brown
   b) strong
   c) sullen

5. Curb
   a) shape into a circle
   b) stretch a canvas
   c) keep under control

6. Erudite
   a) obscure
   b) learned
   c) demanding

Structures

A **Example**   It was a gloomy affair, but it did not distress the hardy Yankees.
It was a gloomy affair, **but not so gloomy as to distress the hardy Yankees.**

1. The children were afraid, but they did not refuse to look at the presents.
2. Andrew's watercolors were good, but they did not satisfy him entirely.
3. He would be interested in visiting the great European museums, but he will not leave Chadds Ford.
4. Some critics say that Jamie is superb, but he will not surpass his father.
5. He was pleased to paint one president, but he did not want to paint another one.
6. They are disturbed by his paintings, but they do not refuse to come again and again.

B   *Transform each "direct speech" sentence below into an "indirect speech," as shown in the example:*

Example   They said, "We will do better next time."
They said **that they would** do better next time.

1. Wyeth said, "I'll try to save Chadds Ford from the advance of Wilmington."
2. N. C. said, "I will not dismantle the Christmas tree until February."
3. N.C. thought, "Experience will give the children a rich background."
4. Andrew said, "I shall do serious work from now on."
5. The critics said, "Jamie will surpass his father."
6. Andrew Wyeth said, "If I travel, I shall never be the same."
7. Nicky thought, "I will be better at selling pictures than at painting them."
8. Andrew told Ralph Cline, "I'll paint you in your old uniform."

Topics for Discussion or Written Assignment

1. What do you think of N. C. Wyeth's theory about the way to enrich the mind of a person? What do you think of his Christmas expedition on the roof and of the effect it could have on his children? What did it do to Andrew? Would you recommend bad or only good experiences?
2. How would you describe Andrew Wyeth?
3. The director of a modern art gallery dismissed Andrew Wyeth as a painter "who does what has been done before." From what you have read about

Wyeth's painting, can you understand in what way that man is (a) right, (b) not quite right?

4. Wyeth's admirers include all sorts of people: young, old, connoisseurs, nonconnoisseurs, simple, and sophisticated. Can you imagine how such different people can be equally attracted to Wyeth's art?

Margaret
Mead

Most anthropologists go about their business without attracting much publicity. One of them may surface in the news, now and then, after discovering a very remarkable piece of bone or disappearing into the unknown, but in general they accomplish their important and exciting work in true scientific fashion—inconspicuously.° This is not to say that Margaret Mead is not a serious scientist; she certainly is—but inconspicuous she is not. First noticed in 1928, when her best seller *Coming of Age in Samoa* came off the press, she has since become as familiar to the general public as an anthropologist can hope to be. She pays for her fame in the usual way and tries to bear calmly the mixture of praise, honor, criticism, and sneers. But it must not always be easy for a spirited woman. After the publication of her second book, one of her colleagues suggested that she had not investigated a particular question. Margaret Mead writes, "I was so enraged° that I got our next field trip postponed° for three months while I wrote *Kinship in the Admiralty Islands* to show the full extent of my knowledge of the subject."

"I have been discussed, ridiculed, and glorified," she says. "I have been called an institution and a stormy petrel,° and cartooned° as a candidate for the Presidency, wearing a human skull° around my neck as an ornament." The skull is undeserved, because a cultural anthropologist like Dr. Mead is not particularly fascinated by ancient bones. Her purpose in life, for the last fifty years, has been to observe the habitual behavior of human beings as conditioned by their culture. In other words, she does not concern herself with the peculiarities° of individuals, but with the habits of whole groups: Indian tribes, Polynesian societies, and even the inhabitants of her own country.

In recent years she has turned her attention to the problems facing the modern world, and her willingness to express her views on questions like race, ecology,[1] and sexual revolution has greatly contributed to her fame. But at the age of seventy she took time off to write, for a change, about herself. It was not

without attracting attention

very angry

delayed

sea bird, supposedly a warning of a storm

humorously drawn

bones of the head

unusual characteristics

[1]Science of the relationship between living things and their natural environment.

for self-glorification. To an anthropologist, the whole of humankind is an immense family, where the experiences of any member can be of help to the rest of the group. And just as she had often used the New Guineans or the Eskimos to instruct her readers, she proceeded to "lay her life on the line,"° in order to show what circumstances had shaped her. Her example, she hoped, would throw some light on "how children can be brought up so that parents and children together can weather° the roughest seas."

lay . . . life) fully expose (her

here, endure, get through

The result is a warm, direct, entertaining book, made all the more pleasant by the author's obvious satisfaction with her lot. She is delighted to be a Sagittarian[2] ("someone who goes as far as anyone else and shoots a little farther"); delighted with her sex ("I was always glad that I was a girl"); delighted with her background ("I have always liked my culture, just as I like my own name"); delighted to have been an anthropologist, to have known love, deep friendships, and motherhood ("Bringing up Cathy was an intellectually as well as emotionally exciting adventure").

Yet she is no Polyanna.° She does not pretend that life has brought her nothing but perfect people and unmitigated° joy. But hurts and failures have their use too, she feels; and this is the point that she tried to make in calling her autobiography *Blackberry Winter.* The title comes from one of her poems, in which she states that the blackberry bushes give more fruit when the blossoms have been exposed to harsh winter frosts.

unrealistic optimist

pure

Incidentally,° it seems that anthropology and poetry go hand in hand. Margaret Mead's books reveal that an astonishing number of anthropologists (including such luminaries° as Ruth Benedict and Edward Sapir) have been dedicated writers of verse. Dr. Mead herself once tried writing poems, and her reverence for poets has involved her in a number of unscientific escapades. Once, for example, she organized a merry expedition in Greenwich Village[3] to hang a basket filled with wild flowers on the doorknob of Edna St. Vincent Millay's[4] house. Another time she and Ruth Benedict found themselves locked inside the Protestant Cemetery in Rome after lingering too long at Keats' tomb.

by the way

famous persons

[2]Person born between November 22 and December 20, in the sign of the Zodiac Sagittarius, "The Archer." Such persons are supposed to be optimistic, honest, sociable, and freedom-loving.
[3]Section of New York City where painters and writers lived.
[4]American poet (1892–1950) most famous in the 1920s.

Margaret Mead counts it as a particular blessing to have grown up in a house where children were treated like adults—with respect. It was a bonus° too, she thinks, to move often and be forced to adapt to new places, new schools, and new faces. The frequent relocations taught her to improvise her "home" wherever she could arrange her few possessions, and to get along with people of different social, racial, and religious backgrounds. Moreover, since her mother believed in taking advantage of local talent to have her children instructed, Margaret was trained in weaving,° music, woodcarving, painting, and carpentry. She was extremely proud, as a bride, to be able to build some of her own furniture herself. She has profited from her experiences in another way. "Looking back," she writes, "it seems to me that this way of organizing teaching and learning around special skills provided me with a model for the way I have always organized my work, whether it has involved organizing a research team, a staff of assistants, or the available informants in a native village. In every case I try to find out what each person is good at, and then I fit them together in a group that forms some kind of a whole."

Little Margaret was conscious of belonging to an unusual family, and when she reached adulthood she realized that she had been brought up two generations ahead of her time. Her mother was a doctor of sociology and an ardent° feminist, "filled with passionate resentment about the condition of women." It made her furious to remember that women were judged unfit to vote, along with criminals and imbeciles.° She had no use for furs or feathers "because they represented the murder of the innocents." She loved to quote poetry, which may account for Margaret's poetic disposition; but it was an odd habit for a woman who was otherwise austere to a painful degree. Margaret's mother seems to have been dreadfully reasonable. Although lovely to look at, she had no coquetry,° "no gift for play, comfort, or pleasure," and no sense of humor; she could not cook, either. At eight, Margaret took over the arrangement of flowers, the organization of parties, and everything in the house that was not strictly utilitarian.° In her teens she often had to run the house and prepare all the meals, while working hard at school. It was exhausting, but she did not really mind too much. She already liked keeping house, and she still does.

Toward her father, who was a professor of economics,

Margaret had mixed feelings. She describes him with clear-eyed affection as unpredictable, imperious,° insensitive to   commanding
other people's feelings, but intelligent and always interesting.
But Margaret owes her ability to analyze situations and her
sense of humor to him, it seems; he also passed on to her his
"enormous respect for facts" and his conviction that the
highest achievement for anyone was to add to the sum of
human knowledge. Margaret disliked his "money-bound
judgments," but she enjoyed his keen mind. "The spring before
he died," she writes proudly, "I gave a seminar to a group who
thought of themselves as avant-garde; but his were the most
searching questions."

The most important person in Margaret's life, the one who
had the deepest influence on her, was her paternal° grandmoth-   related to the father
er, who lived in the Mead household. Grandmother Mead was a
rare woman, a college graduate at a time when girls were rarely
seen on a campus. A former educator, she understood young
people well, and she had definite and advanced ideas on
education. She knew, for example, says her granddaughter,
that too much arithmetic is injurious to young minds, and so
she started Margaret on algebra as soon as the little girl knew
her multiplication tables.

Except for kindergarten, Margaret did not go to school until
she was eight. In that family of teachers, everyone "disapproved of any school that keeps children chained to their
desks, indoors, for long hours every day." It was grandmother
Mead who took care of Margaret's education, who told her
"wonderful" stories, made her memorize poetry, and taught
her everything from botany° to the easiest way of peeling a   science of plants
tomato. She encouraged her to observe. The child was hardly
eight when Mrs. Mead made her keep notes about her two
younger sisters' speech habits. She kept her free from social or
racial prejudice, as well as from any feeling of inferiority about
her sex. Mrs. Mead's example was enough to convince
Margaret that a woman can live comfortably with brains and
that it is perfectly all right to be a girl. In fact, Margaret actually
felt that it was *better* to be a girl. Her own younger brother was
frail and shy, and her father's family tree seemed loaded with
"charming, no-count° men" and "stern, impressive women."   worthless
Nothing there to make her feel inferior. But she did not approve
of her mother's bitterness. And as she grew up she tried not to
become an aggressive feminist, for she had been much more

Margaret Mead   147

Margaret Mead at sixteen

inspired by her grandmother's femininity° than by her mother's feminism.° "It was my grandmother," she writes gratefully, "who gave me my ease in being a woman."

womanly quality
defense of women's rights

    The worst memory that Margaret Mead has from her youth is her first year in college, at De Pauw University in Indiana. Nothing in her broad-minded upbringing had prepared her for the pettiness and the snobbery of the sorority° system as it was then practiced at De Pauw. With astonishment, she discovered that all social life on campus was regulated by these residential clubs, and that only the conventionally acceptable girls were asked to join them. Margaret did not fit at all. She was too intellectual, too unusual. She did not chew gum; she had brought a tea-service with her; she wore strange clothes; and she looked a fright° in the party dress that she had designed herself—a green and silver skirt representing a wheat field with poppies, and a blue and white blouse symbolizing a cloud-strewn° sky. "The idea was romantic," admits Dr. Mead,

college women's club

very ugly

scattered with clouds

148

"but the dress was dreadful." She was judged undesirable. She did not mind not having dates, since she was already engaged to a theology student, Luther Cressman. But it hurt terribly to be constantly humiliated. She reflected that "this was no way to organize society. Both those who reject and the rejected suffer irreversible° damages."

that cannot be undone

The rejection moved her to display her worth. She distinguished herself in class: she wrote, she designed, she organized the school show, she went vigorously and effectively into campus politics, and she was chosen for the English Writing Society. By the end of the year, the sororities were inclined to forget the poppy dress, but it was too late. Margaret had made two observations: first, that adolescent girls mature° faster than boys and outshine° them academically (as grandmother had said); and second, that girls who outshine boys don't charm them much. Since she definitely wanted good relationships with the opposite sex, it seemed wise to transfer to a women's college, where she could be intelligent without worrying about the feelings of young men. The same line of thought inspired her later to arrange her career in order to avoid competing with touchy° males. At first she limited herself to the study of women and children. There was no danger there. Anthropologists agreed that women researchers could do better than men in that field, since it required close contact with native women, which was dangerous for men.

develop physically and mentally
here, surpass, do better than

sensitive

Margaret transferred from De Pauw to Barnard College in New York, where she received her Bachelor of Science degree, with a double major in English and psychology, in 1923. In September of that year she and Luther were married. She kept her maiden name (as she was to keep it through two more marriages). She was following the expectations of her mother, who had given her no middle name so that she would not be submerged° in matrimony and always could preserve her own personality. The young couple settled in an apartment near Columbia University in New York. Luther was studying sociology and working part time as pastor of a small church; Margaret was preparing her master's thesis, dreaming of the time when she would be a minister's wife with six children. Both she and Luther were looking forward to a busy future in a rectory° full of little people and of parishioners° clamoring for comfort and wisdom. It was not quite enough for Margaret, though; she needed to make some other kind of contribution.

drowned *(fig.)*

house of a minister or priest/
members of the church

Margaret Mead   **149**

Since the social sciences appeared to be the most promising field, she had—hesitantly—chosen psychology. Work was already well advanced on her psychology thesis when she happened to take a course in anthropology, which was taught by a pioneer in the field, Dr. Franz Boas, and by his assistant, Ruth Benedict. Margaret, fascinated by the personalities of her two professors, was eventually to become a close friend of Ruth Benedict. But she was equally charmed by the subject of the course. "The reconstructions of Stone Age men with bundles of sticks in their arms had a tremendous power to move me," she recalls, "as they evoked the millennia° it had taken man to take his first step toward civilization." Anthropology it would be, as soon as she had her master's degree. There was something urgent and important to accomplish there.

periods of a thousand years

II

Fifty years later, Margaret Mead remembers her first marriage as "an ideal student marriage," hard-working and lighthearted, enriched by the constant flow of friends who came to enjoy Margaret's hamburger hospitality and to report the ups and downs of their love lives. But it was doomed from the start, for as soon as she had received her master's degree in psychology, Margaret began to feel the pull of the career she had chosen. She was eager to engage in field work.°

scientific work done in a natural setting

Anthropologists seldom operate in New York City. Not that New Yorkers would not make engrossing° subjects, but it is easier to study the fundamental human nature in a "simple" society where man's comportment° is not confused by the interaction of more complex cultural, social, and historical factors. Hence the anthropologists' habit of taking their notebooks and their tape recorders to remote corners of the world, praying all the way that they get there before the primitive peoples have been civilized beyond recognition.° Primitive ways of life are vanishing rapidly. "When I was a graduate student," writes Dr. Mead, "I used to wake up saying to myself: 'The last man on Raratonga who knows anything about the past will probably die today; I must hurry.' " Luther sympathized with her impatience. He encouraged her to accept

extremely interesting

behavior

beyond . . . . so much that they cannot be recognized

the grant[5] that Franz Boas was securing for her from the National Research Council. And to make the decision easier for her, he accepted a fellowship[5] that would keep him busy for a year in Europe.

There were not many women anthropologists in the wilderness in 1925. Worried about the dangers that would face Margaret in "uncivilized" surroundings, Professor Boas tried to talk her into studying adolescence among the American Indians, who were relatively close. Margaret's own choice was to investigate cultural changes in Polynesia. They compromised: she agreed to study adolescent girls on a "safe" Polynesian island—one of the Manu'a Islands of Samoa, which was occasionally visited by a naval vessel. There she spent nine months collecting information. At first it was bewildering.° very confusing Since anthropology as a science was still in its infancy,° it had babyhood no established methods, and Margaret, who had never been taught anything but theories, had to invent her own system. She had to learn the language rapidly, to adapt herself to the Samoan way of life, to the food, to the complicated etiquette,° rules of polite behavior to taking a shower in public. She also had to decline, as kindly as she could, the marriage proposal of a friendly Samoan who had noticed with interest that "white women have nice fat legs." Margaret took it all in stride,° and finally left the island took . . . reacted without difficulty with a wealth of material, very pleased with her first expedition. As she was coming home triumphantly with her booty, she met aboard ship a young psychologist from New Zealand, Reo Fortune, with whom she started a very enthusiastic friendship.

Back in New York, Margaret Mead joined the staff of the American Museum of Natural History as assistant curator in the Department of Ethnology.° While working there she used her science dealing with the races of people notes from Manu'a to write *Coming of Age in Samoa*. The book had been meant to bring the insights° of anthropology to deep understandings the general public; it succeeded beyond her wildest hopes. She also wrote more technical publications based on the same findings. All the while, Luther, who had abandoned theology for sociology, was teaching at City College. There would be no busy rectory after all, and since Margaret had been informed by her doctor that she would never be able to bear children, the

[5]Money given to an artist, scientist, etc., so that he can do a specified piece of work.

whole basis of the marriage seemed to have collapsed. Besides, there was Reo Fortune, who shared her interests. Luther and Margaret agreed to have a friendly divorce, and Margaret married Reo.

The second marriage was to prove less peaceful than the first one. Reo Fortune seems to have been a rather difficult man, who "found it hard to cope with rivalry at any level." He soon became resentful of his wife's growing reputation and popularity. Least of all did he like her attempts to improve his speeches; her suggestions, she says, were "quite realistic but entirely unappreciated." Margaret had some grievances° of her own, one of which was her husband's total disregard° for illness and fatigue. At the end of their second stay in New Guinea, which lasted two painful years, they paid a visit to another anthropologist, Gregory Bateson. As they entered his house, Bateson offered a chair to Margaret, remarking, "You look tired." "I felt," writes Dr. Mead, "that these were the first cherishing words I had heard from anyone in all those months." Eventually she divorced Reo and married Gregory. The third marriage was also to end in divorce, but it brought to Margaret Mead the immense surprise and joy of having a child—her daughter, Catherine, who in time was to provide her with another exciting experience, grandmotherhood.

Margaret Mead has made over a dozen expeditions to the South Sea Islands. She has studied the development of the minds of primitive children, their adolescent years, growth, kinship,° cultural changes, and all sorts of questions related to the effect of culture on sexual characteristics, sexual behavior, and temperament. She has written many books and articles on these subjects, some for professionals, some for children, but most of them for the general public. During the war years she taught at Vassar, lectured in England, wrote a book about the United States (*And Keep Your Powder Dry*), and rose to the position of associate curator of ethnology at the museum. She was also called to Washington to help in the war effort by working with two fellow anthropologists on problems of morale,° communication among allies, and psychological warfare against totalitarian forces. She had just finished a sequel° to *And Keep Your Powder Dry* when the atom bomb was exploded on Hiroshima. Immediately she tore up her manuscript. "Every sentence was out of date. We had entered a new age."

°complaints

°lack of attention

°family relationship

°mental disposition

°work that follows another

Since then most of her attention has been devoted to the difficulties of that new age. Education, mental health, family life, sexual behavior, personality, race relations, the role of women—she has expressed herself forcefully on all aspects of modern society. All her books make fascinating reading, but four of them are of special interest nowadays: *Culture and Commitment* (about the generation gap); *Male and Female* (a study of the sexes in a changing world); *New Lives for Old* (about cultural revolution); and *A Rap° on Race,* which is the conversation, talk (*slang*) text of an extraordinary taped conversation with black writer James Baldwin.

All this time Margaret Mead has been teaching—in most of the major universities of the United States and occasionally abroad. She has lectured widely. She has been curator in the Department of Ethnology (from 1964 to 1969), president of the World Federation of Mental Health, and president of several learned societies. She has received all the honors, medals, awards, and responsibilities that may conceivably befall° an happen to anthropologist of international renown.° She remarks, half- fame amused and half-saddened, that she has become a monument. It is, however, a productive and very lively sort of monument.

What makes Margaret Mead so popular with students, and so interesting even to people who would not know a Iatmul[6] from an Ashanti[6]? She is a superb popularizer, of course. She has many exotic° tales to tell, and she tells them with humor and foreign, strange clarity. But she does not dwell° on exoticism. Most of her put too much emphasis appeal comes from her concern with the future of mankind and with the problems of the world in which she and her audience live. To solve these problems she taps° the knowledge of draws from human nature that she has acquired by studying the primitive societies she calls her "priceless laboratory." From them, she contends, we can learn to understand more and perhaps better ourselves.

Take the Samoans. Among the young girls in grass skirts, Dr. Mead observed that adolescence is not naturally a period of stress, struggle, and delinquency.° Any strain that adolescents wrongdoing have to bear is a product of their society—when that society confuses them with too many choices—and with conflicting standards of behavior—usually their parents' and their peers'. The Samoans, faced with only one way of life, have no such problem. In a more complicated society there would be less of a

[6]Iatmul: tribe of New Guinea; Ashanti: an African people.

problem, says Margaret Mead, if the young were prepared by their educators to cope with the complications. Education is the key to happy adjustment, and as early as 1929 Margaret Mead was insisting that the young should be taught *how* to think rather than *what* to think. It was quite a revolutionary concept at the time. She was also explaining that there would be no conflict if society could become tolerant enough to infuse° its young with the feeling that there is no one ethical° way to live, and that many different sets of values are acceptable.

<small>fill with / moral</small>

Now look at the Arapesh, the Mundugumor, and the Tchambuli of New Guinea. Living with them, Margaret Mead discovered that many of the differences in character between men and women are not inherent° to the sexes. Like adolescent distress, they are a product of social patterning. The Arapesh men and women, who have never heard that they should be different, both present the same meek,° selfless, passive attitude, the same "maternal" devotion to the children. Their passivity bored Margaret Mead, who found them "intellectually aggravating."° But she really disliked the Mundugumor, who do not see any temperamental distinction between male and female either, but who are all equally brutal, devious,° sexually aggressive, and downright mean to each other through life. Even love is fierce, the children unwanted, often killed at birth, and ill-treated when allowed to grow up. As for the Tchambuli, they do expect men and women to act differently, but in their culture it is the men who are sweet and decorative, while their efficient, unsmiling, and unadorned wives take competent care of business.

<small>belonging to, inborn</small>

<small>mild, patient</small>

<small>very annoying</small>

<small>not direct</small>

Why, asks Margaret Mead, do we build artificial standards where nature does not impose any? And it is not only a matter of sex; we make patterns for every category of people. The individuals who do not fit into those patterns have no choice but to resign themselves to a life of maladjustment and misery. It would be much wiser to drop arbitrary standards and to let each individual act according to his or her temperament and abilities, rather than to some fixed idea of what befits his or her sex, race, social background, or any other characteristic.

Many changes are needed, concludes Margaret Mead, if we are to survive. And those changes must be accomplished soon, "because the twentieth century is an emergency for all mankind." We have to revise practically all aspects of our

Margaret Mead with Manus mother and child, Admiralty Islands, 1953.

culture—family life, education, religion, marriage. But there is no reason to be afraid of change, adds Dr. Mead. It can be done painlessly, as the Manus have demonstrated.

The first time Margaret Mead visited the Manus in 1928, they were savages with bushy hair and G-strings° who had no idea that the rest of the world was not living in the Stone Age. Actually, they did not suspect that there was such a thing as "the rest of the world." They discovered it when scientists, missionaries, Australian administrators, and a million or so American GI's° found things to do on their island. The Manus, having considered carefully the ways of their exotic visitors, decided that they were not all bad. In twenty-five years, under the leadership of one man whom Margaret Mead rates as a genius, they transformed themselves from "savages" into a twentieth-century people. They clipped their hair, built solid

<small>small pieces of cloth worn around the hips</small>

<small>soldiers, sailors, and so forth</small>

Margaret Mead

houses, organized local government, vaccinated[7] their babies, started education and health services, adopted the use of money, and stopped beating their wives—as Manus etiquette had hitherto prescribed.° They happily reported to their friend   ordered
Margaret, when she visited them recently, that they were pleased with their peaceful revolution.

We could restyle ourselves just as successfully, says Margaret Mead. She points out that in the first place we should be as intelligent and open-minded as the Manus, who looked at a very alien° culture without assuming, as we too often do, that   foreign
it was surely inferior to their own. She also points out that they did not go in for shallow changes, such as the importing of Coca-Cola, blue jeans, or rock music. They underwent a complete rethinking of their culture. Finally, the changes were not adopted only by the young generation, but by all the Manus at the same time. Together they started on a new path, and together they have weathered the rough seas of cultural revolution. All three generations moved together. What they have done, the people of the United States or of any other "advanced" country can surely do . And the Americans should be able to lead the way; after all, most of their ancestors had to restyle themselves when they immigrated, didn't they?

And so Margaret Mead goes on writing, speaking, and enjoying the sympathy and the affection of a large public. But harsh comments are sometimes heard from the ranks of her fellow anthropologists. Dr. Mead, they object, flies too high, does not stick to proper scientific methods, and, in other words, talks too freely about too many questions that do not come under her discipline. Are they right? Is she? She says that anthropology is now more concerned with the study of change than with ancient customs; that it is a science that protects the future by looking backward. The modern world could do worse, no doubt, than to listen to this seasoned° anthropologist   here, experienced
with a superior, subtle, and daring mind.

---

[7]To inject a substance into the body in order to prevent disease.

Questions

1. What does a cultural anthropologist study?
2. Why is Margaret Mead so widely known?
3. Why did she write about herself?
4. Why is she so pleased to be a Sagittarian?
5. Why does she think it was good for her to move so often?
6. What kind of a woman was her mother?
7. In what ways was Margaret's education unusual?
8. What did Margaret's grandmother give her, besides an education?
9. Why was she unhappy at De Pauw University?
10. Why did she transfer to Barnard College?

Vocabulary

A   1. What is a stormy petrel?
    2. What is a Polyanna?
    3. What is a sorority?
    4. What do you call the science of plants?
    5. What do you call a thousand-year period?
    6. What is the difference between femininity and feminism?

B   *Change the following sentences, using, instead of the verb in italics, the adjective or verbal form in parentheses. Add forms of the verb* **to be** *and prepositions as needed. Read the new sentence aloud.*

    Example   She is *known* to the general public. (familiar)
                  She is **familiar** to the general public.

    1. She *knew* that she belonged to an unusual family. (conscious)
    2. Women *cannot* vote, men thought in the nineteenth century. (unfit)
    3. This may *explain* Margaret's poetic disposition. (account)
    4. Too much arithmetic *harms* young minds. (harmful)
    5. Margaret *admired* her grandmother's femininity. (inspired)
    6. He *resented* his wife's growing reputation. (resentful)

C *Repeat the following sentences, replacing the word or phrase in italics with one with similar meaning taken from the list.*

unmitigated	enraged
luminary	unpredictable
mature	outshine
ardent	inconspicuous
peculiarities	lay on the line
irreversible	imperious
weave	irreversible

1. You cannot say that Margaret Mead is *not easily seen*.
2. She is not interested in the *unusual characteristics* of individuals.
3. She *exposes* her life *fully*.
4. She has not experienced only *pure* joy and perfect people.
5. Her mother was a *forceful* feminist.
6. Her father had a *commanding* personality.
7. Unfortunately, the damage *cannot be undone*. (*is* + *adj.*)
8. Her grandmother had said that girls *do better than* boys of the same age.

Structure

Example   She does not have dates, but she does not mind.
She does not mind **not having dates.**

1. They do not attract publicity, but they do not mind.
2. They do not have the right to vote, but they do not mind.
3. We do not see the poppy dress, but we do not mind.
4. She does not study arithmetic, but she does not mind.
5. I do not know the Mundugumor, but I do not mind.
6. We are not invited to the party, but we do not mind.

Topics for Discussion or Written Assignment

1. Do you believe that there is some truth in astrology or not?
2. Is it better to go to a coeducational school or to a school that is not? Why? Do you agree with Margaret Mead on the problems of coeducation?
3. What do you think of the attitude of Margaret Mead's mother toward furs and feathers? Should hunting and fishing be forbidden and all animals protected? How? Have you ever done anything in favor of animals?

4. In your opinion, what are the good and bad points of the kind of education that Margaret Mead received at home? What is your idea of a good education? What is your idea of the ideal school?

Exercises for Section II   *pp. 150-156*

Questions

1. Why don't anthropologists operate in New York, Chicago, or Paris?
2. What does it seem to be like for a young anthropologist to start field work on a primitive island in a remote part of the world?
3. What kind of questions did Margaret Mead study during her visits to the South Sea Islands?
4. Which of her books can you name, and what subjects do they treat?
5. Why is she interesting to people who are not particularly keen on anthropology?
6. What is interesting about the Arapesh and the Mundugumor?
7. What do you know about the Tchambuli?
8. What does the culture of those three tribes show?
9. What happened to the Manus?
10. Margaret Mead admires the way they conducted their transformation. Why?

Vocabulary

A   *Chose the most accurate of the three words or phrases.*

1. Engrossing
   a) enriching
   b) deceiving
   c) interesting

2. Infancy
   a) small child
   b) Spanish princess
   c) babyhood

3. Morale
   a) mental disposition
   b) set of customs
   c) a sense of what is right

4. Inherent
   a) mad
   b) belonging to
   c) meaningless

5. Alien
   a) somewhere else
   b) foreign
   c) equal

6. Infuse
   a) fill with
   b) interest
   c) bewilder

B *Fill the blanks with nouns suggested by the verbs, nouns, or adjectives in italics.*

Example She was convinced that men are weaker; her father's family tree seemed to justify that **conviction.**

1. She is very *satisfied* with her lot; her _____ shows plainly in her book.
2. She gathered useful *information* from the native _____.
3. Her mother was *resentful* of the condition of women, and she used to express her _____ ardently.
4. The sorority system seemed *petty* to Margaret; nothing had prepared her for that kind of _____.
5. She considered the sorority girls *snobs* and despised their _____.
6. The Mundugumor *infants* are treated without tenderness; life is harsh even in _____ in the tribe.
7. Margaret Mead has *exotic* tales to tell, but she does not dwell on _____.
8. After seven months among the *passive* Arapesh, Margaret Mead was thoroughly bored with their _____.

C *Write the antonyms, using the prefixes* **un-, in-, ir-,** *or* **im-.**

1. Wanted
2. Conspicuous
3. Reversible
4. Fit
5. Predictable
6. Desirable
7. Adorned
8. Sensitive
9. Afraid
10. Smiling

Topics for Discussion or Written Assignment

1. What do you like or dislike about Margaret Mead?
2. Did she convince you that the difference in character between men and women is not natural?
3. What changes would you suggest for our society (marriage, religion, laws, social structure, political organization, and so on)?
4. How do you feel about anthropology? Is it interesting? Important? Why?
5. Do you think that it is possible, in a Western civilization, for all the generations to change together? Justify your answer.

Frank Lloyd
Wright

Born June 8, 1869
In Richland Center, Wisconsin
Died April 9, 1959

When he died at ninety, it was almost a surprise. It had seemed that he would live forever, young, active, and outrageous, to thrill and shock generation after generation of more ordinary mortals. He had announced once: "Not only do I intend to be the greatest architect who has yet lived, but the greatest who will ever live. Yes, I intend to be the greatest architect of all times." A man who disposes so easily of Michelangelo and of Ictinos[1] can hardly be expected to stand in awe of his contemporaries. Wright had nothing but scorn for the achievements of the great modern European architects Gropius, Mies van der Rohe, and Le Corbusier, and he was very much put out° when, visiting the International Exhibition of Architecture in New York in 1932, he found out that their works had been displayed alongside his—and on an equal footing!° In his eyes, this was nothing short of sacrilege.° And perhaps he was right in a way; perhaps he did deserve a room of his own, if not as the greatest architect of all times, at least as the one who had opened a new chapter in the history of architecture, and who had revealed to the modern world what functional° beauty in buildings could be.

    offended

    on . . . in a position of equality / disrespect for something sacred

    working, purposeful

It took not only genius but courage to speak of functional beauty around the turn of the century. Architecturally speaking, the period was an opulent° nightmare. Buildings had to be large, complicated, and in a style borrowed from the past or from foreign lands. Private houses looked like English cottages, Italian villas,° Swiss chalets,° French castles, or like a combination of them all. Public buildings pretended to be Greek or Roman temples—and never mind if the Pantheon° does not make an efficient bank and looks lost between a drugstore and a barbershop. To replace such contraptions° Wright offered his own notion of the ideal human shelter: a beautiful, comfortable house in harmony with its setting° and carefully designed around one central idea that gave a feeling of unity to the structure and the details of its decoration. Since they did not look like anything familiar, the public did not know at first whether to laugh or hang the architect. But some people did understand that Wright was offering something

    rich

    elegant country houses / mountain houses

    ancient Roman temple

    here, strange things

    surroundings, location

[1] Architect of the Parthenon in Athens.

original and exciting—not another version of a sixteenth-century palace in Florence, but the perfect twentieth-century dwelling° for Wisconsin or California. house, place to live

Wright bitterly resented any suggestion that he might have been influenced by the work of other architects. He wanted the world to remember that Gropius, Mies van der Rohe, and Le Corbusier had been still in grammar school when he was making architectural history, and that *they* had received their inspiration from *him*. What need did *he* have of inspiration? Genius, he professed, finds all its inspiration in itself. He was even pleased to have had little training in his field, or, as he would say, to have been "spared the curse of architectural education." But he was not entirely a self-made wonder. His sense of beauty and his cocksure° nonconformism were at least overconfident, conceited partially inherited. To quote Wright himself, he had chosen his family with the greatest care.

His father was a well-educated, restless man who had tried law, medicine, and the ministry before devoting himself to his one true love: music. He had hoped to make a living° teaching make . . . earn enough money to live on music to the people of Madison, Wisconsin, but he never met with financial success—a fact that may account for his bitterness and irritability. One day his wife suggested that perhaps he would have a better chance of finding happiness by himself; he took his hat, left the house, and was never seen again. This was unconventional behavior in 1885, but William Wright had never expressed much respect for man-made laws and conventions. As for his wife, she was the kind of person who would prefer a clean break to a pretense of conjugal° married harmony. Twenty-four years later, Frank was to show that he shared her point of view.

Anna Lloyd-Jones Wright came from a Welsh family of farmers and Unitarian[2] preachers: strong people all, hardy, independent, and proud. She was as intoxicated with education as her husband was with music, and she loved beauty. But her taste must have startled the neighbors. In that age of overstuffing,° overfurnishing, and overdecorating, she deep, thick furniture covering believed in uncluttered rooms, bare wooden floors, simple curtains, "simple vases filled with dried leaves." She picked wild flowers and ate natural foods; everything had to be genuine. Frank inherited her distaste for the artificial and the fraudulent.° His main objection to Victorian architecture was dishonest

[2]Protestant religious group emphasizing individual freedom of opinion.

to be that it was "dishonest." The same passion for honesty marked his private life; Wright always insisted on doing what he considered right, even if it meant leaving his wife and six children to run away with the wife of a client. As he never stooped to feign° a remorse° that he did not feel, he was made to pay dearly for his arrogance. But he took what came—derision, scandal, and even jail—head-on° and chin up. After all, the Lloyd-Jones cherished family motto° was "Truth against the world." And when Frank was a young man, his mother had written to him, "If you ever have to choose between goodness and truth, choose truth, because it is closest to the earth; in earth there is strength." *(pretend / regret)* *(head-first, bravely)* *(saying giving a rule of conduct)*

In the summer, Anna sent her son to his uncle's farm, in the hope that he would develop some muscles, along with a measure of self-discipline and a taste for hard work. Frank never worked up much enthusiasm for farm labor, but he did acquire a strong body, which looked athletic and elegant to his last days, and a deep appreciation of nature. He remained a country man all his life. He loved the soft hills of Wisconsin as later he would love the Arizona desert. And as a builder, he always refused to deface° or dominate the landscape. It was wrong, he repeated, to plant buildings on the top of a mountain. Man was not nature's master; he should try to be her friend and to associate with her by blending his shelters with her rocks and plants. This he tried to achieve even on small suburban lots.° His own home, Taliesin, was built near a hilltop—"not *on* the hill, but *of* the hill." *(spoil the appearance of)* *(small pieces of land)*

When his father disappeared, sixteen-year-old Frank had to go to work for a local contractor,° but he also managed to study engineering and geometry at the University of Wisconsin. The work was an excellent preparation for the practice, if not the art, of building. And Frank, more than anything else, wanted to be a builder. Strangely enough, the independent Wright does not seem to have resented the fact that his vocation° had been preplanned for him. Long before he was born, Anna had already decided that she would have a son who would become a great architect. To force fate, she looked at pictures of English cathedrals all through her pregnancy° and later pinned them on the walls of the nursery. She provided Frank with toys and books that could encourage his interest in architecture. She was particularly inspired when she gave him his first set of *(man who provides workers and material to build houses)* *(chosen profession)* *(period before having a baby)*

Froebel blocks—a type of educational toy that is common now but was quite revolutionary at the time.

The set created by the German educator Froebel included wooden blocks cut in neat geometrical shapes, cardboard° circles and triangles, strips and sheets of smooth and rough paper, all in beautiful colors. With the set came detailed instructions to help children familiarize themselves with forms, colors, and textures, and to teach them to combine the elements in a variety of structures and patterns. Enchanted, Frank played with the set for years. He claimed in his autobiography that the feel of the soft maple° blocks had never left his fingers; nor did he ever lose his liking for geometrical forms and decorations. Some of his early houses looked as though they had been made of Froebel blocks; and he kept experimenting all his life with circular, triangular, hexagonal,° and diamond-shaped buildings.

thick, stiff paper

light-colored wood of the maple tree

six-sided

Perhaps it was Anna who gave her son the *Dictionary of Architecture* by the French architect Viollet-le-Duc, and Victor Hugo's *Notre Dame de Paris.* Those books were among Frank's favorites. He was particularly impressed by Viollet-le-Duc's opinion that the shape of a building should be determined by its function, rather than by the fashion of the day or the fancy of the architect. Excellent idea, but who was putting it in practice at the end of the nineteenth century? Hugo had written a surprising chapter on architecture in his novel about Notre Dame; among other things, he maintained that the native Gothic style[3] of the French cathedrals had been far superior to the imitations of Greek temples favored since the sixteenth century. And young Frank tended to agree with him.

After two years of construction work and engineering classes, Frank came to the conclusion that Madison did not have enough to offer to an eager young man "dreaming architecture." Having sold his father's books and his own fur collar to finance his expedition, he took the train to Chicago. It was his first look at a big city. He had never seen such an ugly place before. With no experience and no recommendations,° young Frank found that landing a job in an architectural firm was much more difficult than he had imagined; but on the second day he did get hired by a well-known conventional

here, letters of praise

[3]Style of architecture common in Europe from the twelfth to the sixteenth centuries.

architect, a specialist in the "cottage style": James Lyman Silsbee. He learned much from Silsbee about the practical aspects of house design: he even became very good at designing cottages. But before long his attention was caught by the work of a rather young architect named Louis Henry Sullivan. At the first opportunity he offered Sullivan his services, was accepted as a draftsman° and thus embarked° on a seven-year association with the man he was to call his *Lieber Meister* (Beloved Master), and whose influence was the only one he ever acknowledged.

person who draws plans and sketches/started

Actually, it was not so much an influence as an encouragement. The two men were meant to understand and to help each other. Sullivan, who specialized in large buildings and skyscrapers, was considered an odd fish° in the profession. Instead of disguising his department stores or his auditoriums as antique monuments, he let them stand boldly for what they were: big practical structures, planned to serve their purpose efficiently behind façades decorated with carved foliage° and arabesques.°

strange, different man

leaves

curving lines

II

Sullivan had the annoying habit of lecturing everyone about the necessity of creating a sensible "American" architecture. Wright, however, was not annoyed; he approved. He quoted Hugo; he quoted Thoreau and Emerson, who had predicted that soon America would reject the influence of its European tutors and find its own taste at last. He talked endlessly with Sullivan about the new native style to be invented. In 1893, Sullivan designed a transportation building for the Columbian Exposition of Chicago. It was the only construction there that was neither neo-Roman, neo-Etruscan, nor neo-anything else. Wright had worked on the building with enthusiasm. But the visitors to the fair admired only the pseudoclassical buildings they were used to, and Sullivan and Wright lamented° together that public taste had been ruined for another century.

expressed deep sorrow

When Frank married pretty Catherine Tobin in 1891, Sullivan presented him with a five-year contract and enough advance cash to build himself a house in Oak Park, a conservative suburb of Chicago. Since the firm did not design private residences, the contract provided that Wright would work after office hours on the few houses that clients occasionally requested; he would of course be paid by the firm. His houses met with flattering success. If not revolutionary, they were different enough, in their simplicity, to catch the attention of would-be homeowners with a slightly adventurous taste. Soon they came directly to Wright with commissions° that he could not afford to refuse. His family was growing rapidly. Besides, he and Catherine were living in the grand manner that Wright was to maintain all his life—whatever the state of his finances. He dressed superbly, rode beautiful horses, filled his home with precious rugs and grand pianos. The only way to pay at least part of the bills was to work furiously.° When a displeased Sullivan discovered that his protégé° had been taking commissions outside of the firm, the two men quarreled, and Wright left. He was not to see his *Lieber Meister* again until the 1920s, when Sullivan was dying, alcoholic and forgotten.

Wright was twenty-one when he had his name painted in gold letters on the door of his own studio. "I longed,"° he wrote later, "for a chance to build a sensible house." Not only were the fashionable mansions° of the day unsensible and pompous,° but "they lied about everything." They had fake° fireplaces in seldom-used parlors, doors that seemed made for giants, false columns, multitudinous gables,° turrets, porches, and doodads;° they had useless attics° and unwholesome cellars. It took Wright several years to polish his notion of what a sensible house should be. After some striking creations, such as the simple, slightly Oriental Winslow House in Chicago, he arrived at what is now called the Prairie House.

Wright wanted to build dwellings that would be shelters— not expensive mausoleums° to show off, but homes offering protection, privacy, and a chance to "enjoy the quality of living." The surviving Prairie Houses still look beautiful today. They are long, low structures, with repeated horizontal lines in the roofs, the terraces, the ribbon of windows, the elements of the walls, even sometimes the built-in furniture.

For the people who lived in them, one of the great charms of the Prairie Houses was the sense of space and freedom that they gave indoors. Wright usually centered the building on a high-ceilinged living room, with a massive fireplace backed by the kitchen, so that all the pipes and flues° could be hidden together in one block. Around that solid core,° the living space

---

orders for work

violently; *here*, very hard

person who has a protector

earnestly desired

large, impressive houses / self-important, exaggerated

false

pointed ends of a roof
useless decorations / spaces under the roof

monumental tombs

passages for smoke

center, heart

Frank Lloyd Wright

spread in all directions with a minimum of partitions° and walls
doors. "I declared the whole floor as one room," he boasted in
his autobiography. What is important, he explained to his
clients, is not the combination of walls, ceilings, and floors but
the living space that they enclose. He was a master at handling
that space so that every part of the house would be beautiful
and surprising, and in merging° it with the space outdoors combining
through a succession of porches, terraces, and gardens. The
house seemed to spread into the countryside—the vast
American prairie. To further blur° the line between "in" and confuse, make indistinct
"out," Wright always tried to build the walls with local stone.
This, he proclaimed, was "organic architecture," an architecture "harmonious in all parts," consistent° with its function, in agreement
with the nature of the material employed and of the
surroundings, and with the personality of its users.

Wright was proud of having made his houses comfortable for
all; even the servants had rooms near the kitchen instead of
three flights up. All the elements were scaled to human
proportion. Typically, Wright had taken his own height as a
standard, and since he stood only 5 feet 9 inches, legend has it
that his tall clients bumped their heads every time they went
through a door. But one should perhaps remember that very
few of the many stories about Wright are true.

By 1909, Wright had become the leading architect in North
America. His works still made the ignorant laugh, but he had
more commissions than he could handle, and he was widely
admired by professionals, particularly in Europe. At home,
architects had been impressed by some of his tall buildings,
such as the Unity Church of Oak Park and the Larkin building
in Buffalo. Both had proved that he could handle vertical space
as masterfully as horizontal living rooms. Many of his
innovations,° such as the H-shaped floor plan of the church, new ideas, inventions
have been copied ever since.

In spite of his success Wright was not enjoying perfect
happiness. For one thing, he was permanently in debt.
Although this did not distress him unduly,° it was annoying. more than it should
He did enjoy his fame, his house, and his six beautiful children.
But his marriage had turned cold, and he was now in love with
the wife of one of his clients, Mamah Cheney. Catherine simply
refused to hear of a divorce. Depressed, overworked, and annoyed, tormented/
harassed° by his creditors,° Wright decided at the end of 1909 persons to whom he owed money
to put an end to his problems. Having made financial arrange-

ments for his family, he fled to Europe with Mamah. They stopped first in Berlin, where an important study of Wright's works was being prepared for publication; then they settled in Italy. In 1911, they came back to the United States as discreetly° quietly as they could.

Discretion, they found out, was out of the question.° Not only out . . . entirely impossible had the scandal been enormous, but Wright's attitude now made it worse. Arrogant and undiplomatic as ever, he informed the world that neither he nor Mamah could have a bad conscience for having done the right thing. A candid affair was cleaner than a loveless marriage, and besides, his private life was nobody's concern. The declaration did not endear the two persons who do wrong / sinners° to the press or to the public. Now a villain,° not to be evil, wicked man trusted even professionally, Wright found that clients had become scarce. Only a few loyal friends were standing by him in addition to his children and his mother. His son John came to live and work with him on the "ideal" projects he was designing in order to keep busy, and Anna gave him 200 acres of land she had inherited from her family in Wisconsin. There Wright built his new home, "on the brow of the hill," and named it Taliesin, which means "shining brow" in Welsh.

In 1913, Wright felt fortunate to have received an important commission for an open-air restaurant and concert park in Chicago, the Midway Gardens. The buildings were just finished and Wright was inspecting the work on July 4, 1914, when he was called from Taliesin: a demented servant had killed Mamah, her two children, and three other persons, and set fire to the house, which was completely destroyed with all its treasures. The stricken° Wright did not receive much hurt, broken sympathy; it was felt that he was getting a just reward for his sins. But a certain Miriam Noel wrote him comforting letters, and when Wright met her she impressed him with her dramatic beauty and her sophistication.° As Catherine had finally agreed knowledge of the world to a divorce, he married Miriam in 1923, at midnight, on a bridge over the Wisconsin River. It was a very romantic start for an absolutely disastrous marriage.

During those lean years of the 1920s Wright created one of his most famous buildings—the Imperial Hotel in Tokyo. He had accepted the commission with enthusiasm, for Japan was a country dear to his heart. During his first trip there in 1905, he had been delighted by the refined simplicity of the Japanese, in which he found a confirmation of his own tastes. Wright, who scorned all works of art, made an exception for the Japanese, and he became an expert collector of Japanese prints. Unfortunately he lost many in the Taliesin fire and was forced to sell most of the rest to survive during his long battle against Miriam.

The Imperial Hotel was an engineering marvel, all the more impressive for being built on a bed of soft mud. It turned out to be as earthquake-resistant as Wright had promised. He achieved this feat by keeping all the elements of the huge structure independent of each other, so that any of them could move without causing the collapse of the whole. The concrete° floor slabs° and the concrete walls barely touching them were cantilevered on concrete pins, which means that they were not supported at their ends but only at the middle. The floors and walls of the Imperial rested on their pins, said Wright, "like a tray rests on the fingers of the waiter." The arrangement provided more flexibility° than a rigid° foundation, and the Imperial did take the severe earthquake of 1923 like a well-built ship takes the heavy seas—riding the waves. It emerged undamaged, restoring Wright's professional reputation.

The appearance of the Imperial Hotel was not as unanimously praised as its stability was. A fascinating masterpiece for some, it looked clumsy,° confused, and overdecorated to most people. What is certain is that it did not look Japanese; if anything, it was Mayan,[4] which is not very surprising, since Wright professed great admiration for the architecture of the pre-Columbian° Mexicans. He found it in complete harmony with its setting; moreover, it was the real native architecture of America, wasn't it? The few houses that Wright built in California after the Imperial Hotel had the same Mayan flavor, and like the hotel they were made of concrete.

Wright loved to use the "natural" materials—stone, wood, and even bricks. But with wood, stones, and bricks one can only build "boxes"—cubic buildings supported by vertical posts and horizontal beams. Wright loathed° the rigid post-and-beam box that, according to him, was never meant to serve life. And he had become increasingly interested in the strength and plasticity° of concrete. This, he thought, would allow a different type of construction: houses without angles

concrete° / floor slabs° — stonelike building material / broad, flat surface

flexibility° / rigid° — ability to adapt / stiff, unbending

clumsy° — not graceful

pre-Columbian° — before the discovery of America by Columbus

loathed° — hated, had contempt for

plasticity° — ability to be shaped

[4]Of the Maya, members of an early, highly advanced civilization in Central America.

172

and corners, wrapped in a continuous skin of poured concrete that would be floors, walls, and ceilings all in one. In short, people could have the kind of home that the snail enjoyed. Wright always considered shells, especially sea shells, the most perfect dwellings in the world, for beauty as well as for functionalism.

It was going to take some years and some technical progress before Wright could realize his ideal buildings. The California houses, made of concrete blocks, were massive, cold, and still very boxy, and Wright had loaded some of them with carved decorations in the art nouveau manner. He was definitely not at his best during those "Miriam" years. But who would have been, considering the chaos° of his private life? complete confusion

III

Miriam, who had seemed interestingly eccentric at first, had proven unbalanced—to say the least. She was to die insane in 1930; until then she used her considerable energy and cunning° to harass her husband and to provide the scandal skill at deceiving and scheming sheets with all the scandalous news they could print. Although she had left Wright after a few months of marriage, she was infuriated by the presence at Taliesin of his new love, Olgivanna Milanoff. Even after their divorce in 1927, she kept giving wild press conferences, forcing her way into Wright's home to smash things, trying to have Olgivanna thrown out of the country and to prevent her former husband from working—all the while making extravagant financial demands. Once she even succeeded in having Wright jailed. Meanwhile, Anna Wright died, Sullivan died, Taliesin, just rebuilt, burned a second time, and Wright had to borrow heavily to replace it. Taliesin III was barely livable when he fell behind on the payments on his loan; the bank foreclosed° and expelled him canceled the loan from his home. At that point, wrote Wright in his autobiography, "the sense of humor was beginning to fade."° disappear

For all his courage, he may not have been able to bear all his disasters with such fortitude° if he had not been so well strength of mind supported. But Olgivanna, whom he married in 1928, was a strong, serene° woman, a former student of the mystic[5] Georgi calm, undisturbed

[5]Person who seeks God and truth through meditation and spiritual and physical exercise.

Kaufmann House ("Falling Water"), Bear Run, Pennsylvania (1936). Designed by Frank Lloyd Wright.

Gurdjieff at the Institute for the Harmonious Development of Man (in Fontainebleau, France). She provided a good anchor in the storm. In addition, Wright's ever-loyal friends advised him to turn himself into a corporation to solve his financial problems. They took shares in Wright, Inc., and raised enough money among them to pay his debts; whereupon the bank, mollified,° allowed him to return to Taliesin. There, in 1932, softened he founded the Taliesin Fellowship, which is still in existence.

The Fellowship was not a school of architecture but a community in which young would-be architects willing to pay a reasonable fee could share in the "natural" life of the master, work on his projects, and listen to his usually outrageous comments on events and personalities. Several hours every day were reserved for absorbing the principles of organic architecture. The rest of the time, the apprentices° had to work in the garden, attend to the Taliesin cows, repair the house, cook the

persons learning a trade or craft

174

meals, and generally serve the Wrights and their guests. They attended the Sunday concerts and helped prepare elaborate° festivities. The rules of conduct were strict: an apprentice bold enough to smoke, to show up for tea in casual clothes, or to cast the smallest doubt about his enthusiasm for community living was sure to face a stiff reprimand° from Olgivanna, or expulsion if he had been bad enough. Most of the students would not have dreamed of rebelling. They felt privileged to participate in an unusual and exciting experience. Like the Wrights themselves, they saw the Fellowship as an island of wisdom in a sorry world. Many remained for years and eventually became associate architects. But it has often been remarked that not one great architect has ever come out of Taliesin. It may be that the proportion of great talents is small in any group, or that only mediocre men could stand the overpowering personality of the master and the total submission and loyalty that he demanded. By dismissing the few young men who dared question his ideas on architecture or on the art of living, Wright may have deprived° himself of the very students who could have done him credit.°

    complicated

    stern reproof, "talking-to"

    taken away from
    done . . . added to his reputation

    The creation of the Fellowship marks the beginning of Wright's triumphant comeback. During the 1930s his works were praised again and exhibited again in several cities, and he was asked to participate in the International Exhibition of Architecture in New York. Displeased as he was to find his designs displayed with those of "ordinary" builders, Wright was forced nonetheless to notice what a younger generation of foreign architects had been doing in Germany, in Holland, and in France. And perhaps he let the severity of their modern architecture influence him in spite of himself, for the houses he built after the exhibition were simpler than his California ones and free of decoration. From that period date some of his most elegant and popular buildings, such as the Kaufmann House in Bear Run, Pennsylvania, and the Johnson Tower in Racine, Wisconsin.

    The Kaufmann House was so admired, so commented on, and so photographed that Wright grew bored with it and complained that it was distracting from his more recent buildings. It is a dramatic house, hanging over a waterfall with bold cantilevered slabs of concrete holding its terraces above the water, while nature gets even,° so to speak, by thrusting a boulder through the floor of the living room. Just as striking in

    pays back

Frank Lloyd Wright

its way is the fifteen-story Johnson Tower. Not surprisingly, Wright thought of tall buildings in terms of nature—sturdy trunks held firmly in the ground by their roots. The trunk of the tower is a massive concrete shaft° enclosing all the pipes, wires, ducts,° and elevators; from it sprout° the cantilevered floors like so many branches, and around this skeleton are wrapped the walls made of alternating bands of brick and glass. The sleek, elegant tower was such a hit that the directors of the Johnson Wax Company happily declared that it was worth two million dollars in publicity. People were constantly coming to look at it, comment, take snapshots, or apply for a job inside.

From the 1930s also date the Usonian Houses, whose name came from a word invented by novelist Samuel Butler for the *United States Of North America* (with an unexplained *i* thrown in for good measure). They represented Wright's attempt to create inexpensive dwellings that could provide "simplicity with dignity." Although they look like smaller Prairie Houses, they were better adapted to the realities of a modern life without opulence and without servants. To cut costs, Wright replaced the garage by a novelty—the carport, and the dining room by another invention—a dining area off the kitchen. The house rested on a concrete floor which floated on a bed of gravel° and enclosed the heating pipes. With a heated floor, an air-conditioned roof, wood walls that needed no paint and no decoration, the Usonian Houses were not only comfortable and beautiful but inexpensive to maintain. They offered many pleasant surprises in the organization of the space and the distribution of light. Altogether they remain one of Wright's most appealing creations. But not all Usonian Houses had to be modest in size and cost; Wright's own Taliesin West, the winter home he built for himself near Scottsdale, Arizona, is a Usonian House on a grand scale. To a guest who was criticizing some details, the laconic Mies van der Rohe muttered during a visit, "Just thank God that it has been built."

The modest Mies van der Rohe admired Wright and recognized easily all that modern architecture—and he himself—owed to his conceited colleague. Wright allowed that he liked Mies, but without approving of his buildings, much too bare for his taste. But then he did not approve of anybody's architecture. He could not find a kind word for the "flat-chested" buildings of the International Style, for those "glassified filing cabinets" in which men were supposed to live

column
pipes for air /
grow up or out

small rocks

anonymously, in neat order, each in his aseptic° compartment. pure, free of germs
True, the international architects had first been inspired by
Wright's own principles, and they claimed to be his heirs. But
they had not accepted his idea of marrying buildings and
nature; on the contrary, they were usually doing their best to
keep them apart. They had also rejected all ideas of decoration
on their glass, steel, and concrete structures. Their buildings
looked all alike, interchangeable—in Wright's view, contempt-
ible. His worst adjectives seemed to be reserved for the
American architects and the American Institute of Architects,
the A.I.A. "Philip Johnson," he would say of one of his most
able competitors, "is a highbrow; a highbrow is a man educated
beyond his capacity." Such witticisms did not make him
popular among professionals, and he was never asked to
participate in important architectural events like the Chicago
World's Fair of 1933, or the New York World's Fair of 1939, or
the building of Rockefeller Center in New York City. Neither

*Main gallery of the Guggenheim Museum, New York (1959). Designed by Frank Lloyd
Wright.*

Frank Lloyd Wright

did he ever receive a commission from the government or from any state.

No matter. By the end of the Second World War, he was recognized beyond any doubt as the Grand Old Man of Architecture. "All you have to do to become a Grand Old Man," he laughed, "is to live long enough." But he admitted without a blush that he was "the greatest architect alive." And he would add, "I defy° anyone to name a single aspect of the best contemporary architecture that was not first done by me." His bitterest enemies had to agree that he was right. Furthermore, he was showing no sign of slowing down. On the contrary, the last fifteen years of his life would count among his most active period of creativity.

challenge, dare

Still searching for plasticity, Wright took advantage of the new materials and techniques at his disposal to experiment with forms. He built hexagonal houses; a diamond-shaped church in Madison, with a roof folded along its median° and raised in front to suggest hands folded in prayer; a circular Greek Orthodox church that looks, with its bright blue roof, like an upturned saucer on a cross-shaped trivet;° the Beth Shalom Synagogue, a hexagonal cone of fiberglass on a triangular base. But the shape that delighted him most was the circle. "Nature knows only circular forms," he proclaimed toward the end of his life. And from nature he eventually borrowed the most perfect, the most continuous shape of all: the spiral. Several of his last buildings are based on the spiral—among them the very famous and very controversial Guggenheim Museum in New York City.

line passing through the middle

support for hot dishes

Wright died on April 9, 1959, as he was seemingly recovering from a minor operation. In his seventy-year career, he had erected almost seven hundred buildings, and of course designed many more. Today some of them look heavy and even old-fashioned, with their art nouveau decoration and their angular built-in furniture. But others, like the Kaufmann House, the Johnson Tower, the Usonian Houses, Taliesin West, the Marin County Civic Center in California, the small Walker House in Carmel, look timelessly beautiful. They are one-of-a-kind buildings, each one meant for its site, its purpose, the life of the people who live or work in it. They are individualistic, and this is what Wright wanted most. In his own words: "Individuality is the most precious thing in life, isn't it?"

Exercises for Section I pp. 164-168

Questions

1. What impression of Frank Lloyd Wright do you get from the beginning of this chapter?
2. What displeased him at the International Exhibition of Architecture?
3. Why could he have deserved a room of his own?
4. What was different between the fashionable houses of the turn of the century and the houses that Wright designed?
5. What does he seem to have inherited from his mother?
6. How did he feel about nature?
7. What is a Froebel set, and what did these sets teach Frank?
8. How did he learn about building in Madison? In Chicago?
9. What important idea of Viollet-le-Duc struck Wright?
10. What could attract Wright in Louis Sullivan's buildings?

Vocabulary

A *Repeat the following sentences, replacing the word or phrase in italics with one with similar meaning taken from the list.*

triangle	put out
disguise	deface
arabesque	setting
hexagonal	spare
head-on	fraudulent
dwelling	feign
cocksure	pregnancy
functional	

1. Wright was very *offended* when they displayed his works with the works of Le Corbusier.
2. He thought that a house should be in harmony with its *surroundings.*
3. He disliked anything artificial or *dishonest.*
4. He refused to *pretend* remorse.
5. He took derision, scandal, and even jail *bravely,* chin up.
6. He did not like to *spoil the appearance of* nature.
7. *While she was expecting her baby* (during her _____) Anna looked at pictures of cathedrals.
8. He built *six-sided* buildings.

Frank Lloyd Wright   **179**

B
1. Who was Ictinos?
2. Who were the great modern architects at the International Exhibition of Architecture?
3. What is the Parthenon?
4. What is a motto?
5. What does a contractor do?
6. What does a draftsman do?
7. Who wrote *Notre Dame de Paris*?
8. What is an arabesque?

True or False

Correct the statement if it is false.

1. Sacrilege is some form of disrespect toward what is sacred.
2. Overstuffing means eating too much.
3. Remorse is repetition of a bad action.
4. A vocation is an oral promise.
5. Foliage means leaves and branches.
6. The maple blocks were made of the dark wood of the maple tree.

Structures

A   **Example**   He cannot admire his contemporaries.
He **can hardly admire** his contemporaries.

1. His contemporaries cannot put up with his conceit.
2. The public cannot understand what he is doing.
3. You cannot blame them for being put out.
4. A Greek temple cannot make an efficient bank.

5. I cannot imagine the Pantheon next to a barbershop.
6. You cannot see the line between *in* and *out*.
7. We cannot imagine how revolutionary the Froebel toys were.
8. He cannot stop playing with them.

B *To the question "What was the reason for his anger?" you can answer simply,
"He did not want the works of other architects to be displayed with his." But
if you want, for emphasis, to repeat, "The reason was . . . ," you must say,
"The reason was* **that** *he did not want the work of other architects to be
displayed with his." Answer the following questions with a sentence starting
with "The reason was . . ."*

1. What was the reason for the public's laughter? (They had never
seen such houses.)
2. What was the reason for Anna's offer? (She felt that her husband
was not happy with her and the children.)
3. What was his reason for selling such precious books? (He needed
money for his trip.)
4. What was his reason for changing jobs? (He admired Sullivan
much more than Silsbee.)
5. What was his reason for studying engineering? (There was no
course in architecture at the university.)
6. What was his reason for leaving the university? (He wanted to
learn architecture at last.)

Topics for Discussion or Written Assignment

1. Do you think that genius finds all its inspiration in itself?
2. Are there some buildings around you (on your campus, in your town) that
you consider particularly ugly or particularly beautiful? Describe them and
explain your opinion.
3. What do you think of Anna Lloyd-Jones Wright's advice, "If you ever have to
choose between goodness and truth, choose truth, because it is closest to the
earth; in earth there is strength"?
4. Have you ever had an educational toy? Do you know any educational toys?
Do you think a toy should be educational? What are the best toys and the
worst toys for children?
5. Do you find big cities ugly? Why? What would a beautiful city be like?

Questions

1. Why were Sullivan and Wright so unhappy after the Columbian Exposition?
2. Why did Sullivan and Wright quarrel?
3. What does Wright mean when he says that the fashionable mansions were "dishonest"?
4. What did the Prairie Houses look like?
5. Describe the interior of a Prairie House.
6. How did Wright "merge" *in* and *out?*
7. Would you like that type of house? Why?
8, What is "organic" architecture?
9. What disaster happened to Wright on July 4, 1914?
10. Why was the Imperial Hotel considered an engineering marvel?

True or False

Correct the statement if it is false.

1. In 1909, Wright was depressed only because he could not pay his debts.
2. In spite of the scandal, he had not lost all his friends.
3. Japanese works of art were the only ones he approved of.
4. A cantilevered element is supported only at one end, but not at both ends.
5. Wright admired the architecture of pre-Columbian Mexico.
6. He was not interested in concrete because he liked only natural materials.
7. Sea shells are functional houses.
8. Wright's ideas were sometimes ahead of the technical possibilities of his time.

Vocabulary

A *Give five words—more if you can—to describe the constructions in which men live.*

B *Choose the most accurate of the three words or phrases to complete the sentence.*

1. A gable is
    a) part of a window
    b) part of a façade
    c) part of a roof

2. A flue is located
    a) inside a chimney
    b) at the top of a door
    c) in the basement

3. The core of a house is
    a) its cover
    b) its walls
    c) its center

4. A creditor is a man who
    a) believes what you say
    b) has borrowed money from you
    c) has loaned money to you

5. A clumsy man is
    a) not intelligent
    b) not educated
    c) not graceful

6. Chaos is
    a) confusion
    b) surprise
    c) noise

Structures

Repeat the following sentences, supplying after each one the proper short question.

Example   They were meant to understand each other.
They were meant to understand each other, **weren't they?**

1. Sullivan was rather annoying with his lecture.
2. He should have known better than to bother everybody.
3. Thoreau and Emerson had predicted that America would find her own taste.

4. Sullivan and Wright worked very hard on the transportation building.
5. Catherine could have asked for a divorce.
6. Wright's first houses seemed rather conservative.
7. But they already had a certain style about them.
8. You would like to see one.
9. By now we are rather curious to see what he built.
10. They should have found a better location for the Imperial Hotel.

Topics for Discussion or Written Assignment

1. Wright thought that he should leave his wife and children because he did not love Catherine any more, and because "marriage without love is a form of slavery, a crime." Do you agree with him? Was he right to leave? Should he have stayed because of the children?
2. Do you prefer to live in a big city or in the country? Why?
3. Wright said: "Early in life I had to choose between honest arrogance and hypocritical humility. I chose honest arrogance, and have seen no occasion to change." Did he make the right choice? Would you advise anybody to follow his example?
4. Do you think that Wright might have been "punished for his sins"? By whom?

Exercises for Section III   pp. 173-178

Questions

1. How would you sum up the story of Taliesin?
2. What sort of woman was Olgivanna Milanoff?
3. What was the Taliesin Fellowship?
4. Why should some of Wright's apprentices have felt put upon?
5. Did Wright keep his best apprentices?
6. Why is it suspected that Wright was influenced by what he saw at the International Exhibition?
7. What is the Kaufmann House like?
8. How do the Usonian Houses compare with the Prairie Houses?
9. Compare Wright's architecture and the international style.
10. Why did Wright consider the circle the perfect form?

Vocabulary

Repeat the following sentences, replacing the blank with a noun or an adjective suggested by the word in italics.

Example   Frank wanted to learn how to *build* houses; he wanted to become a
builder.

1. His comments were usually outrageous but *witty;* unfortunately, his victims seldom forgave his _____.
2. I don't like *angles,* and I find his furniture much too _____.
3. The *circle* being the most natural shape, he designed many _____ buildings toward the end of his life.
4. Wright started a *revolution* in architecture; he was _____ in other fields too.
5. He loved *individuality,* and he was particularly proud of being considered the most _____ architect of the century.
6. Sullivan loved and *protected* Wright, but he was furious when he found out that his _____ was taking commissions directly.

Structure

*Read the following sentences, replacing the blank with **who, whom, which,** or **whose.***

1. In 1923, Wright married Miriam Noel, with _____ he had been living for several years, and _____ had accompanied him to Japan.
2. She had remained with him while he built the Imperial Hotel, _____ he considered one of his most important buildings.
3. After Miriam, from _____ he was divorced in 1927, Wright married Olgivanna Milanoff.
4. Olgivanna, _____ was the daughter of a Montenegrin judge, had lived in Russia and in France.
5. She had been a student of Gurdjieff, in _____ Institute many famous men and women worked, meditated, and learned Oriental dances.
6. The press, _____ was not fond of Wright at the time, described the serious Olgivanna as a "Montenegrin dancer."
7. It was Olgivanna, _____ serenity and rather mysterious beauty sustained Wright through the 1920s, _____ helped him start the Taliesin Fellowship.
8. The Fellowship, _____ is still in existence, tries to continue Wright's work. First the Fellowship's architects did the projects for _____ Wright had left finished designs.

Topics for Discussion or Written Assignment

1. Do you know a person who is a strong individualist? Describe that person.
2. Is individuality the most precious thing in life? Is it useful or dangerous? In what way?
3. If you had a house built, would you choose an architect with a strong personality? Why? Why not?
4. Have you seen the Guggenheim Museum? Describe it. What do you think of it?
5. Discuss the Kaufmann House.
6. Wright ridiculed the idea of building "traditional" houses—copies of old farms, of Southern mansions as seen in *Gone with the Wind*, of English cottages, and so on—in the twentieth century. Do you approve? Do you dislike "traditional" houses? Are they ridiculous, pleasant, beautiful? How do you see the twentieth-century house?

The family of Joseph P. Kennedy at home in Bronxville, New York, November 16, 1937.
Seated, left to right: Eunice, Jean, Edward, Mr. Kennedy, Patricia, Kathleen;
standing: Rosemary, Robert, John, Mrs. Rose Kennedy, and Joseph, Jr.

The
Kennedys

I t all started with Patrick Kennedy, an adventurous young farmer from County Wexford, who sailed from Ireland to Boston in the fall of 1848. For the thousands of Irish immigrants pouring into the United States at that time, life did not turn into a heavenly dream the moment they stepped out of their ships. The only kind of work available to them was backbreaking and underpaid,° and the living conditions in the slums of East Boston, where the newcomers piled up, were not particularly favorable to the pursuit of happiness. Only the hardiest survived. Patrick Kennedy, being young and determined, managed to endure as a cooper° for about ten years—long enough to put down roots and raise a family. He died of cholera° at the age of thirty-five, still poor but leaving three daughters and one son, Patrick Joseph.

The destinies° of the family took their turn upward in the hands of the second Patrick Kennedy. He was the quiet sort, young Pat was.° Cool, purposeful,° dignified, he did not drink, did not smoke, did not talk more than he absolutely had to. He had left school early to help his mother, as a responsible lad should; and he must have been heroically thrifty because, working as a stevedore° on the wharf, he saved enough money in a few years to buy himself a small saloon.° Much care and shrewd thinking led him gradually to acquire more saloons, a wholesale° liquor business, and some shares in a coal mine and in two banks. Modest banks to be sure, but solid; one of them was the Columbia Trust Company. All this did not add up to an ostentatious° fortune. But it was sufficient to make him feel secure, to move the family to a better street, to indulge in a boat (the first Kennedy boat), and to send son Joseph to Harvard. Pat Kennedy had no taste for ostentation; he believed in substance. What he was after was power, and he well knew that the two keys that would give him access to it were money and politics. As his talent for listening, advising, and lending a hand in time of need had made him a respected and popular figure in East Boston, he had no difficulty entering public service. He served on several commissions, was elected to the Massachusetts House of Representatives when he was twenty-eight, and went to the state Senate a few years later.

Margin glosses:

not paying enough money

man who makes barrels

spreading, often fatal, disease

future, fortunes

young . . . *sentence structure often used by the Irish/* having definite goals

man who loads and unloads ships

bar, place that serves liquor

in large quantity

showy, impressive

In Boston around the turn of the century,° financial and ^{around . . . years just before and after 1900} political success was the most an Irishman could expect to achieve. A clear-headed man like Pat Kennedy would not have entertained any illusions about his chances of gaining social recognition as well. The high society of Old Boston—the Boston of the Cabots, the Lodges, and the Lowells—was a fortress closed to newcomers, doubly closed to Catholics, and hopelessly closed to the Irish. No amount of wealth was likely to break the barrier, because the only acceptable money was "old"₁ money, accumulated generations ago by the right ancestors in the proper line of business. Today the Kennedys associate with royalty (and even with Old Bostonians), but then there was no possibility for Pat Kennedy to belong to one of the distinguished clubs, or for his son Joseph to join one of the prestigious° fraternities at Harvard. ^{highly regarded, very famous}

Neither, for that matter, could the rotund° and colorful mayor ^{round, fat} of Boston, John F. (Honey Fitz) Fitzgerald, hope to see his beloved daughter Rose make her debut° with the heiresses of ^{presentation to society, usually at a ball} the Old Society. In Honey Fitz's view, Rose was well above such company anyway. She was beautiful, poised, and brilliant. She could converse as intelligently in French and German as in English. Since the age of fifteen she had often served as official hostess for her father, with all the desirable tact and grace. She had a good head, Rose; she was the apple of her father's eye.° But why did she have to fall in love with that ^{apple . . . precious to her father} red-headed, cold-eyed son of Pat Kennedy? What future did she have with him? For seven years the chagrined° mayor did ^{sadly disappointed} his best to divert° Rose's attention toward more promising ^{turn in another direction} suitors. Given her strong character, however, the undertaking was doomed° to failure from the start, as Honey Fitz must have ^{fated, condemned} known. But when Rose and Joseph were married in 1914, he was not objecting any longer, for after much borrowing and maneuvering,° his new son-in-law had just bought control of ^{careful, delicate operating} the Columbia Trust Company, making himself, at twenty-five, the youngest bank president in the state of Massachusetts.

Joseph Kennedy had been well trained by his father. Along with a strong religious faith and a healthy belief in the virtue of hard work, he had received from him the motto that he would later pass on to his own children: "Come in first; second place is a failure. And don't make mistakes." Pat Kennedy did not have to worry. His Joseph was not the type to settle for second best; nor did he make mistakes in his chosen field. He was, in the words of a classmate, "a natural in business the way Caruso° was a natural in singing." Everything Joseph touched turned to gold. But not by chance. Things don't happen by chance, Joseph said; you have to make them happen. His special talent for making things happen was already obvious when he was a student. Maybe he did not shine at Harvard either as a scholar or as an athlete; but one day in his senior year he saw his chance to acquire a venerable° bus at a low price, seized it, and, having somehow wangled° permission to compete with the regular sightseeing tours, he earned five thousand dollars in one summer, driving tourists around Boston.

a famous opera singer (1873–1921)

here, very old

obtained by trickery

It would have been foolish not to take Joe Kennedy's word that he would be a millionaire before his thirty-fifth birthday. In fact, he did better than he had boasted. Boundless confidence and energy, and a set of supersensitive antennae,° enabled° him to be always on the right wagon at the right time. He was in shipbuilding at the beginning of the First World War, in stocks during the booming° postwar years, in moviemaking at the height of the cinema era, in real estate, liquor importing, oil, and gas when they were all at their most profitable. And he was *out* of the stock market at the time of the 1929 disaster. Of all his deals, the most spectacular may be the bold purchase of the Chicago Merchandise Mart, "the largest commercial center in the world," which he bought cheap (as usual) when the Mart seemed doomed. Naturally, he saw to it that the center prospered instead of perishing,° and its value skyrocketed.° At the end of his life, Joseph Kennedy's wealth was estimated at about four hundred million dollars, one of the most comfortable fortunes in the country.

feelers on the heads of insects

gave ability to

very prosperous

dying

soared, climbed steeply

Joe had not endeared himself to everybody on his way. He was a blunt man, bent on getting what he wanted at any cost, and very hot-tempered; one of his daughters once gave him a robe with "Danger! Explosives!" embroidered on the back. A bad loser, a rough competitor, he could be a cruel adversary° at times; and yet, he could display rare generosity and thoughtfulness—finding jobs for distressed people he hardly knew and paying their salaries for years, without their ever suspecting the source of their livelihood.°

enemy, opponent

means to earn money and keep alive

His genius for attracting dollars was matched by his genius for meeting and charming men who were, or would later be, in a position to help him. He met Franklin D. Roosevelt long before FDR's election to the presidency. Their good relations were reinforced by Kennedy's early support of Roosevelt's New Deal, and by his generous contribution to the presidential campaign. In due course,° Roosevelt rewarded his friend's at the proper time loyalty by granting him what Joseph had long yearned for: an official position in the government. The first one, as chairman of the Securities and Exchange Commission, may have been a manifestation of Roosevelt's sense of humor, since the purpose of the commission—to regulate financial operations and the stock market—was to put an end to many of the very business practices that Joe had used during his career. However, he did a fine job, moved on to the chairmanship of the Maritime Commission,[1] and finally, in 1938, was appointed ambassador to Great Britain. His father and his grandfather the cooper would have shared his joy—the Kennedys had now really arrived.

The prestigious ambassadorship meant much to Joseph Kennedy. It added a prominence to his name that money alone would never have provided. He was no more interested than his father in money for its own sake. His tastes were simple, almost austere. As far as he was concerned, family life and good music would do. Money only helped to gain status,° at high social position least outside of Boston. But the Bostonians were left behind in 1929; to take his children away from a place where they would not be admitted in the best circles, Joseph moved his family to a mansion on the outskirts° of New York; later he also acquired a zone surrounding the city residence at Hyannis Port on Cape Cod and a villa in Palm Beach, Florida. All three houses were large, comfortable, happy, and unpretentious.° The favorite was Hyannis Port, not showy where the whole family gathered when Joseph was not away on business. It is still "home" for the clan.° large family group

Joseph Kennedy had another good reason for building up his fortune. He wanted his children to be free from the annoyance of making a living, free to devote themselves to higher endeavors, preferably in the field of government. To insure their independence, even from himself, he set up several trust funds that would give each one of them ten million dollars. In the meantime, they were not to be spoiled by his wealth. Kennedy banned° money as a topic of conversation, particular- forbade, excluded ly at the dinner table. And Rose kept them literally counting

[1]Commission created in 1936 to develop and maintain a national merchant marine.

pennies by giving them meager° allowances. When John F. thin, small
Kennedy became President of the United States, the press
delighted in publishing the formal request he had submitted to
his father, at the age of eleven, to have his allowance raised
from forty to sixty cents a week. The President was not at all
sure that his fervent plea had met with success.

Both Joseph and Rose were excellent parents, dedicated first
and foremost to the upbringing of their brood.° "The measure children
of a man's success in life," Joseph said, "is not the money he
has made. It is the kind of family he has raised." With pride and
joy he saw to it that his four boys and his five girls counted
among the best: Joseph, Jr., and John, eighteen months apart;
the vivacious° Kathleen; Rosemary—a beauty, but mentally gay and lively
retarded; Eunice; Patricia; and Robert (eight years younger than
John); Jean; and finally Edward, who was eight years younger
than Robert.

They were brought up with a unique mixture of simplicity
and sophistication. The furniture was comfortable and child-
proof rather than precious, the food was plain, and the house
was no more tidy than could be expected with bands of
children and pets running in and out and dropping sand and
clothing at random.° "I remember finding tennis shoes parked by chance, anywhere
any place from beneath the table in the entrance hallway to the
top of the baby grand piano," recalls Rose Kennedy in her
memoirs. But there were servants and nurses, several sailboats
for the boys to race in, and when young Robert tried to
supplement° his allowance by delivering newspapers, he did it add to
in a chauffeur-driven Cadillac (without parental approval,
however). The guests with whom the young Kennedys were
encouraged to share views at the table were cardinals,[2]
diplomats, financiers, movie stars, politicians, and world-
famous personalities in all walks of life. The girls were
educated in the best convents. The boys attended nonreligious
schools (including Choate, a renowned Episcopal preparatory
school), because Joe thought that they would get a broader
outlook° by having contact with people of various religions point of view
and backgrounds. After high school all four boys went to
Harvard University; Joseph, Jr., and John were also sent during
the summer to the London School of Economics, to study under
the famous socialist economist Harold J. Laski. Not that Joseph,

[2]High officers of the Catholic Church; members of the group that elects the
pope.

Sr., condoned° socialism, but he was sure that some day one of   approved of
his boys would find it useful to be thoroughly acquainted with
the arguments of "the other side."

The boys traveled extensively in Europe, South America,
North Africa, Russia, and the Orient. Robert visited Mongolia
with Justice William Douglas. And while Joseph, Sr., was
ambassador, the two eldest boys worked in the American
embassies in Paris and London for a while—it was all part of
the training.

Above all, they were trained to compete ("Win, win, second
best is a loser!"): to push themselves as hard as they could,
particularly in areas where they were not gifted. When he
became attorney general, the shy and stammering Robert
would force himself to make speeches, rehearsing fiercely until
he became tolerably good. Their father always urged them to
strive° for excellence and to keep in mind that "much is   try hard
expected from those who have received much." He did not
have to tell them to stick together against the rest of the world;
all the Kennedys were proud of each other, concerned with
each other, and ready to take care of their own. Rosemary was
kept in the family until, at twenty-three, her condition made it
necessary to move her to more serene surroundings. Until then
she was lovingly involved in all the activities, taken as a crew
member in one of the boats during competitions, included in
the dancing parties, and presented to the king and queen of
England between Rose and Kathleen.

"My father was not around as much as some fathers when I
was young," said John F. Kennedy once. "But whether he was
there or not, he made his children feel that they were the most
important thing in the world for him." They were, and he knew
how to make each one feel loved and respected. He also knew
how to build their confidence. "If I had fallen on my face, my
father would have only said, 'The way you picked yourself up
was very graceful,'" said John. And while he was struggling
through a difficult campaign in 1960, he was to say again: "As
soon as I do anything, there is Dad saying: 'Smartest move you
ever made!'"

II

Joseph strove to keep his sons' minds independent. He did
not like them to always agree with him. At the dinner table,

during discussions, he always made a point° of taking the view opposite to the one they were developing, and he was delighted when they argued with him—even more delighted when they banded together against him, and when Joe, Jr., who had his hot temper, would stalk out of the room in anger, slamming all the doors he could find on his way.

made a special effort

With Joseph away from home a great part of the time, it fell on Joe, Jr., to act as substitute father for the rest of the family. The role suited his domineering nature very well, but he was gentle and helpful toward the young ones, who accepted his authority without question. With John, who contested it, things did not go as smoothly. The two were constantly fighting, always with the same humiliating result for John, who was much smaller and weaker. Joe was a bit of a bully, an explosive young man full of good spirits who, according to one of his teachers, "couldn't pass a hat without squashing it in or leave an unprotected shin° unkicked." But his radiant smile, his geniality,° his willingness to help one and all compensated for his uninhibited ways, and he was enormously popular. Handsome, confident, brilliantly gifted, he appeared to everyone as the most promising of all the bright Kennedy children, the one obviously meant to be a leader. His heart was set on a political career. There was no doubt in his mind, nor in his father's, that some day Joe, Jr., would become President of the United States.

part of the leg below the knee

friendliness

For John (Jack to the family), following his brother in school after school was a harrowing° experience. He could not compete. At Choate Joe had won the award reserved for the student who best combined scholarly and athletic excellence. Jack hated Choate. An indifferent student, he could not take interest in anything but history. For years it looked as though the future Pulitzer Prize winner would never master the intricacies° of English spelling. One of his problems was his poor health. While his brothers and sisters sailed through the normal sequence° of childhood diseases and broken limbs, Jack was kept in bed for long periods by scarlet fever, diphtheria, and jaundice. In his first year at Harvard he broke a disk in his spine at a scrimmage.° The injury was to plague him all his life, cause intense pain, and eventually force him to undergo two operations that were not entirely successful. Circumstances thus forced him to turn to books, and he became the most avid reader of the family. Although he liked history books and

very painful

complications, difficulties

series

a practice football game

biographies best, he read anything that he could put his hands on. From this supply his unbelievable memory was to draw the unending flow of quotations with which he later laced his political speeches.

Alone at the university after Joe's graduation, John finally blossomed.° Said a professor who knew the whole family: "It was clear to me that John had a far better historical and political mind than his father and his older brother; indeed that John's capacity for seeing current events in historical perspective° and for projecting historical trends° into the future was unusual." A trip to Europe before his senior year reinforced his interest in world affairs. When the time came to write his thesis, he chose to explain the reasons for England's lack of preparation for the Second World War. The thesis, entitled *Why England Slept,* was received *summa cum laude* and published in book form in 1940, bringing to the young author his first literary success, as well as Joseph's enthusiastic approval.

Not too surprisingly, Joseph Kennedy had made a controversial ambassador. He had been a great social success, despite his emphatic° refusal to wear knee breeches° at court, and had even become one of the rare close friends of Prime Minister Neville Chamberlain, whose conservatism and distaste for war he found entirely to his liking. He approved of the Munich pact and of Chamberlain's policy of appeasement° toward Hitler. And he kept urging Roosevelt to keep the United States out of the war. England, he insisted, should be left to follow her own course without participation by the United States. But the President's inclination and the mood of the liberals had veered° from noninterventionism to a serious concern for the Western world. Joe Kennedy found himself painfully out of tune° with his own government. In 1941, after being further embarrassed by the publication of some incautious remarks he had made to a journalist, he had to offer his resignation. He came back home with a reputation of conservatism and anti-Semitism° which did not bother him unduly but which was to make the liberals uneasy about the position of his son John. They need not have worried, for John Kennedy did not share his father's ideas at the time, and Joseph was, as always, proud to see his offspring° stand on his own two feet. It was the fruit of his training.

The United States entered the war in December 1941, and in a very short time three Kennedys were inolved in it. Joe, Jr., left Harvard Law School to volunteer for naval aviation. Jack,

developed

in . . . in relation to history

directions

forceful / eighteenth-century pants, reaching just below the knee

satisfaction by accepting demands

turned

out . . . on a different course

feeling against Jews

child

refused by both the Army and the Navy, set out to improve his physical condition in order to satisfy the examiners. The Navy relented° on his second try, but assigned him to a desk job that struck the new lieutenant as much too sedate° for his ardor. After some string-pulling,° he was put in charge of PT-109, now the most famous torpedo boat of the United States Navy. PT-109 did not remain afloat very long. In August 1944, a Japanese destroyer plowed right into it, killing some of the crew, and sending the rest, skipper° included, into the Pacific. The men swam toward some distant islands. For five hours John Kennedy towed° a wounded member of his crew by grasping the belt of the man's life jacket in his teeth. He led his men to safety, and after five hungry days the message he had carved on a coconut reached the Marines and brought rescue. For his bravery Lieutenant Kennedy received the Navy and Marine Corps Medal. But the ordeal had been too much for his back; he had to be discharged and sent to the Chelsea Naval Hospital near Boston.

And there he was when the news arrived that Joe, Jr., had been killed in the explosion of his plane, during a dangerous mission. The blow cut so deeply into their father's heart that he never fully recovered; he could never bring himself to talk about his dead son, nor to read the book *(As We Remember Joe)* that Jack put together during his convalescence.° As for seventeen-year-old Robert, the shock prompted him to join the action too; he enlisted in the Navy.

At the time of his brother's death, John Kennedy was twenty-seven. The lukewarm° student had long since turned into a reflective, extremely curious young man with a philosophical turn of mind and a detached,° objective way of looking at the world. Although he found politics fascinating, he had never considered entering the field while Joe, Jr., was alive. He was too shy and too reserved to be a politician anyway, and his tastes inclined toward more scholarly pursuits—teaching perhaps, or writing. Besides, Joe would be running for office for years to come and it would never do to have "a whole mess of Kennedys asking for votes." It may not be true that Joseph, Sr., pushed his second son into public life after the eldest died; John himself made contradictory comments on this point. But certainly Joe, Jr.'s, death changed the configuration° of things. In any event, when a congressional seat became vacant in Massachusetts at the beginning of 1946,

gave in
quiet
use of influence
ship's captain
pulled behind him
period of recovery
here, not very serious
not favoring either side
general situation

John decided to take the plunge. A campaign ensued,° the likes ~followed~
of which Boston had never seen, with a flock of Kennedys and
devoted friends ringing doorbells and pouring tea at all kinds
of social gatherings, and with Rose talking to groups of women
about her family, her dead son, or the latest fashions she had
seen in Paris. It had never been done before, but it gathered
votes like magic, and John won handsomely. He was to be
reelected with the same ease in 1948 and 1950. The candidate
was, to say the least, as unusual as his campaign. The
professional politicians of Boston watched with surprised
interest his fresh, low-key° approach—direct, easy, never ~discreet, quiet~
vulgar, never strident.° "A classy° kid," said an old-timer, not ~loud / having elegance and quality~
altogether disapprovingly. "A total political animal," conclud-
ed others.

As a politician, however, John Kennedy was still unformed.
He had ideas; he wanted to serve; he wanted to remedy social
ills and do what he could to avoid another war. But he had no
political philosophy. Not that he could have done much in the
House of Representatives. As he found out to his chagrin,
junior congressmen seldom have the opportunity to transform
the world. In four years, he succeeded only in acquiring a
reputation for courage and independent spirit. He had dared
attack the sacrosanct° American Legion, which had been ~especially sacred~
opposing a much-needed housing project. Worse yet, when
asked to reconsider, he added pluckily° that the Legion had not ~bravely~
had a constructive idea since 1918! Rather than waste his time
in Washington, Kennedy concentrated on keeping in touch
with his constituents° and on making himself known in every ~people who elected him~
corner and town of Massachusetts. By 1952 he was strong
enough to make a bid° for the senatorial seat held by a pillar of ~make . . . try for~
Old Boston society, Henry Cabot Lodge, Jr. Lodge seemed
bound to win; he was sure to win; nobody doubted that he
would win. But he had never yet encountered the Kennedys on
the warpath.° Neatly defeated, he was heard to moan: "It's ~on . . . ready for a fight~
those damn teas! It's those damn teas!"

For Jack Kennedy, the years in the Senate were marked by
private happiness and terrible physical suffering. At the time of
his election he was wooing°—mostly by long-distance tele- ~trying to win in marriage~
phone—a young socialite° of elusive charm and strong ~person prominent in fashionable society~
personality named Jacqueline Bouvier. He won there too, and
they were married in 1953. Jack's best man[3] was brother Robert,
[3]Man who assists the groom at a wedding.

himself married since 1950 to the irrepressible° Ethel Skakel. It *high-spirited, uncontrollable*
could have been a blissful time in John's life if his spinal injury
had not flared up.° By 1954 he was on crutches° and enduring *become violent/long canes supporting a lame person under the arms*
excruciating pains. In 1955 he submitted to two dangerous
operations. He almost died of complications after the second
one, but it did relieve him for a while, until he wrenched° his *twisted, turned violently*
back again during a tree-planting ceremony in Canada in 1961.
He was always in pain afterward. But he did not have
Addison's disease[4], as has often been contended. The adrenal
deficiency from which he suffered was not of tuberculous
nature like Addison's disease; it was less severe, but it did
lower his resistance to infection. During his long convalescence from his second operation, John Kennedy turned again to
literature and history to keep his mind off his pain. With the
help of Jacqueline, who was doing some of the research work,
he wrote *Profiles in Courage*, which received the Pulitzer Prize.
It was a study of the lives of several historical figures who had
displayed the quality he admired most: courage—political or
otherwise.

When 1956—a year of presidential elections—came around,
Senator Kennedy had become a familiar figure in Massachusetts. He had also skillfully managed to win the backing of the
local Democratic machine.° Without any doubt he was one of *here, political organization*
the party's most promising young "possibles." To his surprise,
he almost received the nomination for vice presidential
candidate at the Democratic convention. The defeat was a
blessing in disguise, since the Republicans were sure to
triumph that year with Dwight D. Eisenhower as President. But
his near victory at the primaries made it clear to Kennedy that
he could win next time, and not in the second slot but in the
first one. Almost at once he started to run for President. Soon
Time magazine was reporting that the young senator "was
leaving panting° politicians and swooning° women across a *breathing hard / fainting*
large spread of the United States."

"I suppose anybody in politics would like to be President,"
he said at that time. "It is *the* center of action. . . . At least you
have an opportunity to do something about all the problems
which I would be concerned with, as a father or as a citizen." In
October 1959, in Robert's living room, the four Kennedy men

[4]Disease of the adrenal glands, the glands that supply adrenalin (a substance
that controls blood pressure and breathing).

*Robert and
John F. Kennedy*

(from Joseph, Sr., to Teddy) and a handful of seasoned
assistants devised° the strategy of the campaign for the _{planned, drew up}
primaries. Robert was to be in charge of it all. In 1956 he had
spent all his time at the convention observing the battlefield
and noting how a campaign should, and should not, be
conducted.

Robert had been in large part responsible for the election of
his brother to the Senate in 1952. At the time he was
twenty-six, just out of the University of Virginia Law School,
and investigating cases of tax fraud for the Justice Department.
He quit his job to take charge of John's campaign, which had
started very badly. His experience was nil,° but he made up for _{nothing, zero}
his deficiency with devotion, an abrasive° but effective way of _{rough, harsh}
getting things done, and a superhuman energy. "Jack works
harder then any mortal man," father Joseph would say. "Bobby
goes a little farther." Robert toiled,° coaxed, bullied, pressured, _{worked very hard}
and had his brother elected, but not without starting the
reputation of ruthlessness° that was to follow him to the end of _{lack of pity or consideration}
his life. Yet the bad names he was called did not mean as much
to him as the link that had been forged° between him and Jack, _{firmly formed}

The Kennedy family at Hyannis Port, Massachusetts, November 10, 1960, after the election of John F. Kennedy to the presidency. Seated, left to right: Eunice (Mrs. R. Sargent Shriver), Mrs. Rose Kennedy, Mr. Joseph P. Kennedy, Jacqueline (Mrs. John F. Kennedy), Edward Kennedy; standing: Ethel (Mrs. Robert Kennedy), Stephen Smith, Jean (Mrs. Stephen Smith), John F. Kennedy, Robert Kennedy, Patricia (Mrs. Peter Lawford), R. Sargent Shriver, Joan (Mrs. Edward Kennedy), and Peter Lawford.

a bond that would be reinforced through the years as a maturing Bobby made himself John's wisest and most trusted advisor.

John Kennedy had been an awkward, if charming, candidate during his first campaign in 1946. Now that he had gained confidence, he was a superb speaker—articulate, witty, and elegant without affectation.° He had also matured. From hesitantly conservative he had evolved into a "moderate liberal," an independent, open-minded man, concerned but dispassionate and by nature optimistic. To Jacqueline he had defined himself as "an idealist without illusions." Unlike many idealists, however, he was obviously a "doer," a quality that appealed to young people—so much so that he once suggested jokingly that the voting age should be lowered to twelve!

° unnatural behavior

At the beginning of the 1960 campaign, his main problem was his religion. No Catholic had ever been elected President of the United States. A large number of citizens, particularly in the South and in the midwestern "farm belt," felt very suspicious of all "popish"° candidates, particularly of one who ^{Catholic (derogatory)} was also darkly accused of trying to "buy" the presidency. Kennedy's opponents were confident that the religious issue would sink the Kennedy boat during the first campaign in West Virginia, one of the most stolidly° Protestant states in the ^{firmly} Union. Kennedy, used to facing things squarely, went on television to clear the air. He explained in his cool, measured tone that "when a man stands on the steps of the Capitol and takes the oath of office, he is swearing to support the separation of state and church . . . and if he breaks his oath, he is not only committing a crime against the Constitution, but he is committing a sin against God."

Something in his earnest speech appealed to the sober West Virginians; the resounding° victory they gave him in their state ^{forceful} did much to help him secure the nomination as Democratic candidate. In November 1960, by a very small margin, John F. Kennedy was elected President of the United States over Richard M. Nixon.

III

For the happy half of the nation who had carried John F. Kennedy to the White House, the weeks following the election were a period of immense expectations and wonderment. The press and the public watched in fascination as the young President prepared for his task with enthusiasm and "vigah."° ^{"vigor" as pronounced in New England} It was a time of glamour and high spirits. There was Jackie, graceful and aloof.° There was a whole flock of Kennedys and ^{cool and distant} assorted consorts,° all handsome, all frightfully active. There ^{husbands and wives} was poet Robert Frost reading the work he had composed for the Inauguration—when had a poet been invited to the presidential box before? There was the team of newly appointed Cabinet members—and they too were brilliant, efficient, and young, at least in spirit. They had brains and, like their chief, they had style. There were more Harvard graduates, more Rhodes Scholars, more eggheads per square foot than in any remembered administration. "Even the Postmaster Gener-

al," notes David Halberstam in *The Best and the Brightest,*
"even the Postmaster General had written a novel, albeit° a bad   although
one!"

It lasted less than three years, not long enough for a new
administration to turn its intentions into realities nor to
sustain° what it had launched. John Kennedy had talked of   support, keep going
relieving poverty at home and abroad; of easing° racial   relieving, making lighter
discrimination; of helping new struggling nations; of strength-
ening the friendship between the two Americas; of exploring
the stars and conquering disease. What came of it? What did he
accomplish? He did start the Apollo program that was to land
Neil Armstrong on the moon. The Alliance for Progress was
initiated,° and the Peace Corps sent 20,000 volunteers into   started
forty-six countries. At home, the desegregation laws already in
existence were just beginning to be enforced, painfully, and a
small army of federal marshals forced the University of
Mississippi to accept its first black student. A civil rights bill
was sent to Congress for approval in June 1963.

But John Kennedy would not be there to see the bill passed in
1965. Neither would he be there to keep the Alliance alive nor
to cope with the general unrest of the late 1960s.

Nobody can say how he would have approached the problem
or how he would have dealt with the Vietnam situation. His
most heartfelt concern had been to insure peace in the world. In
that area he had made some progress after an initial fiasco:° the   failure, disaster
Bay of Pigs disaster, in April 1961. The invasion of Cuba by
Cuban refugees had been planned during the preceding
administration and promoted by the CIA; but Kennedy, who
had failed to cancel it, shouldered the blame. As bad luck
would have it, he had been scheduled to meet Nikita
Khrushchev in Vienna in June, a bare two months after the
fiasco, when his prestige was at its lowest ebb.° An   decline
unimpressed Khrushchev bullied and threatened. In August
the Berlin Wall went up; in September Russia resumed nuclear
testing. In October it was discovered that Russian missiles were
being installed in Cuba.

The week of anxiety that followed can be considered
Kennedy's toughest and finest hour, as he slowly chose the
course that would convince his adversary of his firmness and at
the same time let the embarrassed Russian leader disengage
himself with a minimum of difficulty. His skill and courage
paid off; the Russians removed the offending weapons and the
crisis subsided.° In July 1963, Russia signed the Nuclear Test   calmed down

Ban Treaty she had been turning down° for four years. Slowly, refusing
hesitantly, cautiously, the mood was changing on the
Russo-American Cold War front. A measure of understanding,
perhaps of trust, was established. What would have come out of
that fragile détente° is a moot° question, for when he put his
name on the treaty, John F. Kennedy had no more than four
months to live. On November 22, 1963, he was assassinated in
Dallas, Texas, by an embittered ne'er-do-well° named Lee
Harvey Oswald.

improvement in relations / open to discussion

worthless person

Quite a few people resented John F. Kennedy enough to
rejoice at his death. But the great majority, inside and outside
of the United States, mourned him as they would a cherished
member of their family. Poor people, rich people, potentates,°
whites and nonwhites, friends and ex-foes° for once cried
together. Even the crusty° Soviet Foreign Minister Andrei
Gromyko was seen shedding tears in the American Embassy in
Moscow. Robert F. Kennedy did not let himself be caught
weeping. He took care of his brother's funeral and of the family
arrangements with more efficiency and briskness, if possible,
than usual. But he was deeply hurt, possibly the most deeply
hurt of all. His whole world had collapsed, and in the months
following the assassination he came very close to collapsing
also.

rulers, heads of state

former enemies

tough

Robert worshiped his brother. He had never had it in him to
do things by halves. He hated with passion ("Just like me,"
Joseph would say), but those he loved—his brother, his
madcap° Ethel—he loved with absolute devotion. He was an
intense man, much more emotional than the cerebral° John. He
remarked once that if he had not been a Kennedy, he might
have become either a juvenile delinquent or a revolutionary
priest. It would have well suited his moody, melancholy,°
lonely temperament, and his need for total dedication.°

impulsive, irrepressible

directed by the brain

sad by nature

devotion, commitment

Since 1952, most of Robert's life had revolved around his
brother. Kept apart until then by the age difference, they had
discovered each other during John's senatorial campaign. For a
short while afterward, they had gone their separate ways: Jack
had entered the Senate, married Jacqueline, and gone through
the ordeal of his operations. Robert had been hired as counsel
for the Senate subcommittee headed by Joseph McCarthy, the
notorious demagogue° whose wild anticommunist campaign
disrupted the country in the early fifties. Robert did not dislike
McCarthy, who was an old friend of his father's, but he
disapproved of his high-handed° methods and of his total

politician who appeals to emotions and prejudices

rough and unjustified

disregard for the truth. He left the subcommittee after six months. A few months later he was chief counsel for the McClellan "Rackets" Committee, doing his utmost to uncover proof of corruption in the Teamsters'° Union. The man he wanted most to get was Jimmy Hoffa, the smart, tough, unprincipled president of the union. To the puritanical Bobby, Hoffa represented evil incarnate.° He went after him with single-minded determination. He could not see such a man with the cool antipathy° that John would have felt; he hated him, and the feeling was mutual.° Before he could have Hoffa indicted,° he had to quit his job to handle his brother's presidential campaign. And at the time of Hoffa's conviction, in 1963, Robert was past caring. Jack was dead; nothing mattered much any more. He barely muttered "Good job" to the assistant who had finally cornered his old bête noire.°

> truck drivers

> in human form

> strong dislike

> shared by both sides

> charged with a crime

> person particularly disliked

While winning his brother's trust and the campaigners' admiration, Robert had also earned the loathing of a host of people everywhere. He was impatient, rude, and generally in too much of a hurry to give a thought to the toes he was crushing on his way. Why bother? "I don't care," he would say, "if anybody around here likes me, as long as they like Jack." People considered him not only ruthless but immature. The judgment puzzled his friends, who knew him as a different person—gentle, supersensitive, and so painfully shy that at business luncheons he had to hide his shaking hands under the table. "Bobby," chuckled° a close friend, "Bobby has a heart like a marshmallow."

> laughed softly

After John Kennedy's election in 1960, neither Jack nor his assistants could imagine the presidency without Bobby at work somewhere in the wings. After much agonizing, the President decided to make him attorney general.[5] The cries of nepotism° and the complaint that Robert was not qualified for his job had been anticipated. John Kennedy joked about the nomination: "I don't see what's wrong with giving Robert some legal experience before he goes out to practice law!" Privately, he commented more soberly: "What if he does happen to be my brother? I want the best men I can get, and they don't come any better than Bobby."

> favoritism toward a family member

As it turned out, Robert Kennedy became not only a fine attorney general, but a very important man in the government, and one of the coolest in time of crisis. It was he who found the

[5]Head of the Justice Department; the highest legal office in the United States.

way to deal with the Cuban crisis, who always came with unvarnished° facts, well-considered advice, and enough courage to present unpopular ideas. McGeorge Bundy, special assistant for national security, was to explain after Robert's death: "In the Cabinet . . . I can remember times when he would deliberately° put himself in one of the smaller chairs against the wall rather than seem to be asserting himself.° But it did not make much difference, because wherever he sat was one of the most important places in the room."

unadorned

on purpose

displaying authority

After his brother's death, Robert found it difficult to readjust to a world that had lost its center. He traveled, he defied death by shooting rapids[6] and climbing mountains. For a while he pinned his hopes on the vice presidency in 1964. When President Johnson made it clear that he would not put him on the ticket, Robert changed his plans. After resigning his post at the Justice Department, he ran for a senatorial seat in New York and was elected in November 1964, amidst a concert of applause, insults, and cries of "carpetbagger."[7] For four years he devoted himself with predictable "vigah" to the needs of his constituency and to the denunciation° of the United States commitment in Vietnam, which he was to oppose with increasing bitterness.

accusation, condemnation

The last four years of his life saw Robert Kennedy evolve from liberalism to his own brand of radicalism; at the end he was positively obsessed° with the problems of poverty and racial injustice. Of course, they were not new to him; he had always advocated social equality and as attorney general he had helped Martin Luther King and the blacks fighting for their rights in the Southern states. He had consulted, rather unsuccessfully, with many prominent blacks. But his head and his moral sense, rather than his heart, had been involved. As a New York senator, he visited the most miserable slums of the city and discovered the grim reality—the stench,° the despair, the children disfigured° by rat bites. Appalled and sickened, he tried in vain to bring about some kind of policy for new housing and jobs for the underprivileged. He visited the rural poor of the South and the migrant workers'° camps in California. The experience proved shattering. He was at times so shaken that, says a witness, "his hands and his head

possessed by one idea

very bad smell

scarred, mutilated

crop pickers who move from place to place

[6]Going down the dangerous, swift parts of a river in a small boat.
[7]Name given after the United States Civil War (1861–1865) to men from the North who came to the defeated South to seek wealth or power. They were said to carry all their possessions in one handbag made of carpet fabric.

trembled with rage. . . . Compassion, anger, and pain mingled° and flattened his features." *joined together*

Many people derided Robert Kennedy then, refusing to believe that his indignation and his anguish were anything but a smart ploy° to get himself elected President. But the *trick, move in a game* dispossessed felt differently; by 1968 he had the trust of the discontented—the young, the aged, the blacks, the chicanos.° *Mexican-Americans* They were getting ready to give him their votes, and if Sirhan B. Sirhan, a young Iranian who had convinced himself that Robert Kennedy was a dangerous enemy of the Arabs, had not shot him to death in Los Angeles on June 5, 1968, it may be that Robert would have become "the President of all the unrepresented people," as he had promised to Negro leader Charles Evers.

Much has been said about the malediction of the Kennedy family: some mysterious curse that took the lives of Joe, Jr., Kathleen and her husband, John, Robert, and many of their relatives, and that showed itself in Rosemary's retardation, in Teddy's near fatal plane accident in 1964, and in the Chappaquidick nightmare.[8] Robert himself had mused° about it *considered thoughtfully* often. In 1964 he was saying: "I don't know that it makes any difference what I do. Perhaps we are all doomed anyway." He certainly felt doomed, and during his last campaign, in 1968, his close friends, like him, *knew* that he did not have long to live. But do curses exist?

Only one of the brothers remains now. There are also the sisters and a score of young Kennedys. And a memory lingers on,° the memory of a brief, happy, hopeful period of sparkle *remains* and impossibly high dreams; a period when a new President would announce that he wanted to help establish "a world which would be safe for democracy and diversity and personal distinction." A time when everybody's future seemed full of promises—Camelot.[9]

---

[8]On July 18, 1969, a car carrying Edward Kennedy and a young woman who had helped in Robert Kennedy's campaign, ran off the bridge at Chappaquidick, Massachusetts. Edward Kennedy failed to rescue the woman, who drowned; the whole episode, including his failure to report the accident immediately, has been the subject of continued controversy.

[9]Legendary location of King Arthur's court; a symbol for something ideally happy and beautiful.

Questions

1. How did the Kennedys come to be Americans?
2. What happened to the first Patrick Kennedy?
3. What did his son Patrick achieve?
4. What do you think of the family motto?
5. Why was Rose Fitzgerald Kennedy an asset for an ambitious husband?
6. How well did Joseph Kennedy do at Harvard?
7. How did he make his fortune?
8. What do you think he considered the high point of his career?
9. What kind of schools did Joseph choose for his children?
10. What was "simple" and what was "sophisticated" in the way the children were brought up?
11. Why did Joseph send his sons to the London School of Economics?
12. What was he training his sons for?

Vocabulary

A   *Repeat the following sentences, replacing the word or phrase in italics with one with similar meaning taken from the list.*

livelihood	in due course
wangle	outlook
rotund	ostentation
enable	at random
wholesale	supplement
condone	chagrined
stevedore	divert
doomed	meager

1. Patrick Kennedy did not like *attracting attention.* (one noun)
2. The mayor was *sadly disappointed* by Rose's interest in Joe.
3. His antennae *gave* him *the ability* to feel the best chance.
4. As children, they received *small* allowances.
5. They dropped their toys and shoes *anywhere.*
6. Robert tried to *add to* his allowance.
7. Joseph did not *approve of* socialism.
8. But he wanted his sons to acquire a broad *point of view.*

B 1. What do you call a man who makes barrels?
2. What do you call a man who loads ships?
3. What do you call the kind of business that sells things in large quantities?
4. Who was Caruso?
5. What are antennae?
6. Where are the outskirts of a city?

Structures

A **Example** He made the center prosper.
He saw to it that the center prospered.

1. Pat made his son go to college.
2. She made the children include Rosemary in their games.
3. He made the company give a job to that poor man.
4. They made the older children take care of the youngest.
5. He made the two boys become familiar with problems of foreign policy.
6. He made his children feel loved and respected.

B **Example** He ordered them to help each other.
He told them **that they were to help each other.**

1. He ordered his daughter to forget Joe Kennedy.
2. Pat ordered his son to come in first because second place is a failure.
3. He ordered the children to stick together.
4. He ordered them to strive for excellence.
5. She told them not to leave their shoes on the piano.
6. He told Robert not to take the car to deliver his papers.
7. He told John not to ask for a raise again.
8. She told the children not to let the dogs in the house.

Topics for Discussion or Written Assignment

1. Consider the attitude of Boston high society when Patrick and Joseph Kennedy lived there. Have you seen such an attitude where you live? Does it exist still, or is it a thing of the past everywhere?
2. What do you think of Joseph Kennedy?
3. What was important in the upbringing of the young Kennedys, and how did it shape them?
4. To build his sons' confidence, Joseph used to praise whatever they were doing ("Smartest move you ever made"). Do you think that this constant praising is always helpful for any individual in any circumstances?

Exercises for Section II   *pp. 193-201*

Questions

1. How would you describe Joe, Jr.?
2. How did John compare with his brother?
3. Why was Joseph Kennedy's ambassadorship not entirely successful?
4. What happened to the Kennedy boys during the war?
5. How did John Kennedy mature in his twenties?
6. How did he win his first elections in Boston?
7. What can you say of his career as a congressman?
8. How did he become a young "possible" in Massachusetts?
9. What gave him hopes for the presidency in 1956?
10. What kind of health problem did he have in the 1950s?
11. What is *Profiles in Courage?*
12. What role did Robert play in his brother's senatorial campaign?

Vocabulary

A   *Choose the most accurate of the three words or phrases.*

1. Geniality means
   a) great intelligence
   b) great imagination
   c) great friendliness

2. Intricacy means
   a) complication
   b) fragility
   c) secret influence

3. Emphatic means
   a) not likable
   b) forceful
   c) understanding

4. Relent means
   a) slow down
   b) give back
   c) show mercy

5. A sedate person is
   a) conceited
   b) quiet
   c) ambitious

6. Wrench means
   a) obtain by trick or force
   b) twist
   c) throw

7. Devise means
   a) plan
   b) guess
   c) counsel

8. An abrasive man is
   a) rough
   b) distant
   c) difficult to understand

B *Explain the meaning of the following sentences by making clear the meaning of the italicized words.*

1. Chamberlain was following a policy of *appeasement* toward Hitler.
2. Kennedy was *out of tune* with his own government.
3. John *pulled strings* to get out of his desk job.
4. He *made a bid* for Cabot Lodge's senatorial seat.
5. Robert's experience in campaigning was *nil*.

Structure

Example He had to act as substitute father.
   It fell on him to act as substitute father.

1. She had to help her son with his mathematics.
2. They had to tell Joe about the death of his son.
3. He had to fulfill his father's ambition.
4. She had to organize teas for women voters.
5. She had to do the research work in the library.
6. He had to convince his audience that his religion would not make any difference.
7. They had to demonstrate that a Catholic could be elected.
8. He had to take charge of the whole campaign.
9. They had to investigate the case.
10. She had to ring doorbells in that part of town.

Topics for Discussion or Written Assignment

1. Is the religion of a politician important today and why?
2. What do you think of politics as a career?

Questions

1. What was so exciting about the new administration in 1960?
2. What did John F. Kennedy want to accomplish?
3. What was realized?
4. What had Robert Kennedy done while his brother was senator?
5. Who was Jimmy Hoffa, and what did Robert Kennedy have to do with him?
6. How would you describe Robert Kennedy?
7. What kind of career did he have when his brother was President?
8. What changed him after he became senator from New York? How did he change?
9. How did he die and why?
10. What do you know about Edward (Teddy) Kennedy?

Vocabulary

A   *What is:*

1. the queen's consort?
2. a détente?
3. a ne'er-do-well?
4. an ex-foe?
5. a madcap?
6. a demagogue?
7. evil incarnate?
8. a bête noire?
9. a stretch of rapids?
10. a migrant worker?

B   *Repeat the following sentences, replacing the blank with a word (adjective, verb, or noun) suggested by the italicized word in the first part of the sentences.*

1. Patrick Kennedy had no taste for *ostentation*, and his son and grandsons were not _____ either.
2. When he was elected, John F. Kennedy *expected* much from his presidency; but it was also a time of _____ for the people who had elected him.
3. The link between John and Robert was *strong* already at the time of John's senatorial campaign; it was _____ by Robert's participation in the government.

4. Rose's *conversation* was amusing, and she could _____ just as well in French, German, or English.
5. One of John Kennedy's *initial* plans had been to help poor people at home and abroad; to that end, he _____ the Peace Corps.
6. Lee Oswald was a *bitter* young man; he had been _____ by his many failures.

C *Repeat the following sentences, replacing the word or phrase in italics with one with similar meaning taken from the list.*

muse	moot
linger on	mutual
albeit	high-handed
melancholy	aloof
ebb	stench
turn down	unvarnished
indict	denunciation
subside	ploy

1. She has a rather *distant* personality.
2. After the Bay of Pigs fiasco, John F. Kennedy's prestige was at its *lowest level.*
3. Slowly, the crisis *calmed down.*
4. Whether or not he would have been able to cope with the new problems is a *debatable* question.
5. Robert had the courage to present the *unadorned* facts to the President.
6. He was shocked by the despair, the overcrowding, and the *bad smell* of the slums.
7. His enemies thought that it was only a smart *trick* to get himself elected.
8. Once he *said thoughtfully* that perhaps there was a curse, perhaps they were all doomed.

Structure

Repeat the following sentences, replacing the blank with a form of **let** *or* **leave.**

1. Kennedy _____ (past) the Cuban refugees go ahead with their plans.
2. He was rather depressed when he _____ Vienna after seeing Khrushchev.
3. _____ me read that paragraph again.
4. Robert did not _____ anybody see him crying.
5. He _____ (past) an assistant pursue the indictment of Jimmy Hoffa.
6. He does not _____ his office until after midnight.

7. He _____ (past) the Justice Department to campaign for a senatorial seat.
8. His death did not _____ him accomplish what he had planned.
9. Robert does not _____ anybody see his hands.
10. He always _____ (past) his children take their risks.

Topics for Discussion or Written Assignment

1. How would you compare Joseph Kennedy, Sr., John, Robert, and Edward (if you know enough about him)? Which one would have made the best President?
2. Was the Peace Corps a good idea? Would you like to join the Peace Corps? What would you like to do if you joined it? Or can you think of a better way to be helpful?
3. Robert Kennedy had talked about being "the President of all the unrepresented people." Would you like to see such a President? What could be expected from him? What could be bad about such a President?
4. Do you feel that there might be a curse on the Kennedy family? Do you believe in curses? Explain your answers.

A 5
B 6
C 7
D 8
E 9
F 0
G 1
H 2
I 3
J 4